FROM TRADITION
TO MISSION

FROM TRADITION
TO MISSION

WALLACE E. FISHER

abingdon press   new york   nashville

to the men and women and boys and girls in
THE LUTHERAN CHURCH OF THE HOLY TRINITY
IN LANCASTER, PENNSYLVANIA, WHOSE LORD IS
JESUS CHRIST AND WHOSE BOOK THIS IS ————

INTRODUCTION

That the church of Jesus Christ is a sleeping giant is now an accepted fact. The church has an enormous membership and still enjoys a large measure of public respect, but it demonstrates, in most areas, only a fraction of its potential influence on our total culture. In countless communities the Christian cause seems to be unwilling to die and yet is unable to recover the secrets of true vitality. The church can continue for a long time in this marginal existence, partly because of human inertia. The doors of the buildings can be kept open, at least on Sundays, and congregations of some kind can be assembled, even when the fire burns low. In particular the church can continue as a marrying and burying society, after its relevance to most aspects of contemporary experience has been lost.

The fact that the church so often fails when it could be exceedingly powerful rather than merely respectable defines, in large measure, our problem. This problem is the conversion of the church. Since most Americans at least *claim* to be affiliated with some church or synagogue, it is obvious that the major field of evangelism must be within the alleged membership. If anyone can show how new life in the existing church is possible, that is great good news.

The value of Dr. Fisher's book lies precisely at our point of need. If we are to know how the required conversion is to take place, we must pay very close attention to the record of actual experience. Almost anyone can speculate about what the local church ought to be and how life can be renewed, but such speculation is worth very little in contrast to the actual record of events.

Operating, as we must, between discouragement and hope, we are immensely heartened by any concrete evidence that vitality has actually appeared. The story of what has transpired and is transpiring in Lancaster, Pennsylvania, is one of the most heartening stories I know. I have seen something of this story at first hand, and I bear witness that the vitality is genuine. The most encouraging single feature is the emergence of the hard core of committed men and women who operate as lay preachers and lay evangelists. Many have dreamed of such a company, but in Lancaster it exists.

Wallace Fisher's book is presented, I am glad to say, in the spirit of science. If we are to have a scientific approach to anything, we must listen to firsthand reports. There is, of course, a place for theory; but we cannot theorize, profitably, in a vacuum. Early in the process we need reports of experiments. The present book is one of several such reports now being made. Another is the account of the glorious experiment of the Church of the Saviour in Washington, D. C., *Call to Commitment*. A third, *In the Midst,* tells a similar story of another denomination, in Cincinnati. If we have a sufficient number of such reports, we shall be in a position to make a true induction. It is hoped that these stories, and particularly this significant account written by Dr. Fisher, will make readers realize how great is the possibility of renewal in the midst of old established congregations which we have so much reason to love. The real success of the experiment will depend on the degree to which others are inspired to seek its repetition.

D. ELTON TRUEBLOOD

PREFACE

No book is ever wholly the work of any one person. Some of this material on parish renewal was shared in lay and pastoral conferences—denominational and interdenominational —throughout the United States and Canada. The response encouraged me to write, enriched the content, clarified the argument. A former professor, Theodore G. Tappert, first suggested this "report from the field." D. Elton Trueblood lighted the fuse for it. Trinity's official board and staff, together with seventy-five or so parishioners and nonmembers in Lancaster and a half dozen of my graduate students at Gettysburg (Lutheran) and Lancaster (United Church of Christ) Theological Seminaries, read an early draft. This mutual counsel— crossing congregational, denominational, and professional lines —makes the report a consensus in evaluating parish renewal at Trinity Church.

The secretaries at Trinity, especially Mrs. Charles D. Flowers, were patient and efficient in preparing the manuscript. Former associates R. Ray Evelan and Ernest G. Werner, and present associates Jack R. Hoffman, Albert F. Mattison, and Hugo W. Schroeder, Jr., and official board members Ralph M. Barley, the Hon. Ruth Grigg Horting, Paul A. Mueller, Jr., Mrs. Elvin M. Musselman, Bruce A. Westerdahl, and Dr. Robert H. Witmer read several drafts, offering invaluable comments. I am similarly indebted to my brother, Carl E. Fisher, an officer in his congregation, and my brother-in-law, George E. Stauffer, a clergyman.

My wife, Margaret, generous about the report and gracious with the reporter, shared her Christian insight and wit in recalling and evaluating these twelve years at Trinity. My debt to her in all relationships outruns any formal acknowledgment. Our son, Mark, was as patient as most twelve-year-olds with a father who dared to write during a family "vacation" at the shore. My unspeakable gratitude for the privilege of serving and being served in Trinity parish is reflected in this account of our life together.

WALLACE E. FISHER

CONTENTS

FROM TRADITION
TO MISSION

PROLOGUE

"The strange thing about the Church is not that it grows old, but that it seems to have discovered the secret of being born again." [1] The increasingly negative attitude taken by many concerned critics of the contemporary parish in the face of its social irrelevance highlights the church's crucial need to discover that secret. But the church is born again only as specific congregations are born again.

Studies in depth of the American parish are a crucial need at this juncture. The late H. Richard Niebuhr stated this need imperatively.

The definition of the Church—even the awareness of its actuality—constitutes one of the main concerns of modern theology. Thus we

[1] Daniel T. Jenkins, *The Strangeness of the Church* (Garden City: Doubleday & Company, 1955), p. 14.

17

have arrived at one of those points where the reform of theological education apparently must wait on the reformulation of theology. Much confusion and uncertainty in theological schools today seems to be due to lack of clarity about the community—the Church; about its forms and matter, its relations and composition. Without a definition of Church it is impossible to define adequately the work of the ministry for which the school is to prepare its students.[2]

A definition of the church—indeed an awareness of its actuality—may not emerge clearly in this generation without depth studies of the parish itself. The parishes are the laboratories of the church where the doctrines of God and man are actually tested, emasculated, or ignored. They are the laboratories where smooth homilies insulate persons against reality, or gospel preaching calls men to repentance and faith; where "snappy" programs sell religion, or evangelical teaching equips the saints to witness in the world. The parishes are the arenas where personages, relating casually to their own kind, escape rugged encounters with God, or acknowledged sinners discern life's true meaning in the personhood of Christ and for his sake render priestly service.

The Nature of This Report

This is a depth study of a particular parish. It is the account of an old downtown church (sixty years older than the United States, located at the heart of an eastern metropolitan area of 285,000 persons) which discovered the secret of being born again. It is the firsthand report of the Lutheran Church of the Holy Trinity in Lancaster, Pennsylvania—a congregation which, standing before the tribunal of biblical evidence, was persuaded

[2] H. Richard Niebuhr, *The Purpose of the Church and Its Ministry* (New York: Harper & Row, 1956), pp. 17-18.

by the Holy Spirit to distinguish between illusion and reality in its corporate quest for authentic ministry. The report demonstrates that, while the impasse between theology and activism in the parish can be broken, the vital congregation does not exist simply by sound theology or by the formal possession of the gospel. It testifies that the church exists by the power of the Holy Spirit through the Word in preaching, teaching, the sacraments, and man's response in commitment to this recurring Event. It views the church as "happening."

The report also testifies that tradition is a proper base for mission. Change for the sake of change will not transform the American parish. Continuity and change go hand in hand. Dynamic conservation and responsible innovation are interdependent. Parish renewal does not scorn the foundations laid by those who labored in yesteryear; it corrects and builds on them. Parish renewal does not berate "faithful members" for their religionized convictions, nor does it manipulate them to produce an efficient institution; it confronts them with the Word, acknowledging and accepting their God-given freedom to respond as they will.

There is frustration and anguish in this elemental address. How could it be otherwise? The spirit of the Lord comes with fire; alienation and reconciliation, rejection and acceptance are the complex results. There is no easy path, no diplomatic way, no neat programmatic approach to parish renewal. The rebirth of a congregation in the power of God comes by pain and travail. Trinity Church, however, is not disposed to dwell on the pain of rebirth but rather to rejoice in its new life of service. We know firsthand that renewal is not man-centered. We remember how often we were too proud to ask, and God gave; too timid to knock, and he opened doors; too bone-tired to seek, and he allowed us to find. That is the primary reason for this report: the glad witness to God's power that renews the parish's exercise of Christ's ministry.

These are the theoretical propositions which Trinity's renewal clothes in actual, reportable events.

The American parish is poised geographically and in the hearts of many people for a relevant witness to God's redeeming love.[3] When it discovers the secret of being born again, it becomes an effective instrument for exercising Christ's ministry in our depersonalized society. Consequently, this report rejects the judgment of those who, convinced that the institutional church cannot be recalled to effective witness in this generation, bypass it in their efforts to share Christ with a lost world. The truth that the unconverted church can perish as a finite center in a perishing finite culture is inescapably clear, but the judgment that its demise has taken place is premature.

The born-again parish does not despise institutional forms. It brings these forms regularly under God's judgment to discern whether or not they are means or ends, altering and discarding those which contribute little or nothing to the parish's exercise of Christ's ministry and devising new forms to carry on his dynamic ministry. Christianity has been able to bridge the centuries by providing a Spirit-inhabited institution through which the Word can become flesh in each new generation. Christ's church shapes historical forms through which Christ can confront persons in time, forms within which it can *be* and through which it can accomplish God's mission. The freedom of the Spirit to persuade men in their freedom to respond to Christ is helped or hindered by institutional forms. The born-

[3] Martin E. Marty, *The New Shape of American Religion* (New York: Harper & Row, 1960), p. 125.

again parish employs, adapts, and devises forms which help rather than hinder. It seeks to fashion a framework in which continuous renewal is possible.

A true sense of Christian vocation emerges and grows among the laymen when, viewed as subjects rather than objects, they are confronted with the Word in their freedom and equipped from it to witness and serve. The laity can be taught to view the priesthood of believers not as a band of spiritual anarchists but as the company of the committed who, accepting God's authority, exercise priestly service to God and man. Thereafter, many can be persuaded to accept this biblical view as authentic and orient to it. Gospel preaching persuades persons to repent and become disciples. Evangelical teaching equips these disciples to be witnesses who render priestly service. Christian vocation emerges "like a melody played by ear in the rhythms of twentieth-century life." [4] It is a fruit of gospel faith and evangelical obedience.

Because the image of ministry entertained and projected by clergy and laity affects radically the degree to which the ministry of Christ is exercised by any parish, it is imperative that the whole congregation lay hold on an authentic image of ministry. The quest for this image begins not within the context of the "profession" but within the context of the faith. Standing under the judgment of the Word, the parish must perceive that the authentic minister (ordained or lay) begins as a man—perverse, finite, lost—justified through faith and made new in Christ, but still a man. God uses this new creature, obedient in his freedom, to communicate the living Word to persons in *their* freedom, equipping responsive persons from the Word to be prophets, teachers, evangelists. Thus the church becomes God's mission.

[4] *Ibid.*, p. 147.

Specifically, the report is on this order. Chapter 1 defines Trinity's historical situation in 1952: a parish knowing the gospel in form but not possessed by it in fact. Chapter 2 tells how the clergy and laity allowed the Word to guide them in distinguishing between illusion and reality in their corporate quest for authentic ministry. Chapters 3 and 4 describe how persons are motivated to repentance and faith by the Spirit through the Word in preaching, and equipped from the Word in teaching and counseling to witness in the world. Chapters 5 and 6 report on the life and work of these lay preachers, teachers, and counselors—their impact on the church and the world. Chapter 7 demonstrates how the born-again parish employs institutional forms in the exercise of Christ's ministry. Chapter 8 describes Trinity's new images and sets forth the conclusions of this report.

The Reporter's Theological Frame of Reference

If the writer owes his reader a forthright statement on why and what he has written, he should also sketch the theological frame of reference from which he writes. It is our testimony that Trinity's renewal roots in the Word of God. But what do we mean, "the Word of God"? Paul Tillich differentiates a half-dozen different meanings for this phrase.[5] Throughout this report we use this term to mean the good news of God's saving work in Christ—the message about the essential nature and purpose of God in every evidence of his dynamic, saving activity, initiated at creation and revealed progressively at his pace through myth, legend, historical events, historical persons (Amos, Hosea, John the Baptist), and preeminently in the his-

---

[5] Paul Tillich, *Systematic Theology* (Chicago: University of Chicago Press, 1951), I, 157.

torical person of his Son, Jesus Christ. We accept Scripture as the inspired but uneven witness to God's saving activity. But "if the Scriptures themselves, as a whole, claim to be the Word of God, they can be this only if they are, as a whole, interpreted in terms of Christ. . . . Christ is Lord of the Scriptures." [6] This report of God's saving activity is more than a report; and the Christ-event, rooted in a precise moment of history, is not bound by history. The message of Christ, as Luther observed, "is to me not simply an old song about an event that happened 1,500 years ago . . . ; it is a gift and bestowing that endures forever." [7] Wherever a community of people accepts the authority of God's Word and shares it through preaching, teaching, and the sacraments, Christ confronts persons as he did in Galilee. Exercising their "dreadful freedom," some accept their given place in the new community; some, almost persuaded, decline to pay the cost of discipleship; some, loving darkness, work diligently to extinguish the Light. The church, happening, is engaged relevantly with the world.

This book takes issue with the current disposition of the American parish to rely on programs, methods, techniques, and human personalities as substitutes for the Word's confrontation of persons through persons. Methods do not produce motivation. Motivation invents or borrows adequate methods, varying according to the situation. The born-again congregation, motivated by the Word, will adapt, borrow, and invent the necessary methods and mechanics to communicate relevantly its source of new life. A fresh awareness of the relevance of God's Word, a

[6] Martin Luther. Quoted in an unpublished lecture, "Word of God, Sacraments, and Ministry," by T. G. Tappert, professor of church history, Lutheran Theological Seminary at Philadelphia.

[7] *Ibid.*

growing disposition to search the Scriptures with Christ as guide, a healthy regard for and critical interest in theology, a fresh examination of and unqualified commitment to the biblical images of the church and its ministry, a new awareness that the offense of the gospel breeds tension, conflict, and personal suffering—these are needful in the parish if there is to be spiritual rebirth.

Congregations can be stirred to parochial "activity" by skillful managers and promoters, but no congregation will be born again and nurtured in its new life without converted people— ordained and lay—who allow God's Word to confront others through their persons, accepting their share of hardship as integral to rebirth, spiritual growth, and relevant witness. Until the church's ministers know from the common faith *and* their own experience of Christ that only God's Word can shatter natural man's illusions about himself, motivate repentance, offer forgiveness, make him a new creature, and bestow the gift of eternal life; and until the love of Christ constrains them to make that witness, the world will dismiss the parish as being irrelevant.

────CHAPTER 1────
THE STATELY DOWAGER

I do not envy those who will carry the banner of Christianity in the twentieth century. . . . Yes, perhaps I do, but it will be a stiff fight.
—MARCUS DODS

Trinity Church, the oldest church in the oldest inland city in the United States, was the dowager among the churches of Lancaster, Pennsylvania. From the vantage point of impressive age she disdained any suggestion for change offered by a few of her children and, like most dowagers, basked in the glories of yesteryear. Stately, impressive, able to inspire nostalgia, Trinity Church was indisposed to involvement with rapidly expanding metropolitan Lancaster in 1952. And "Old Lancaster" sustained

"Old Trinity." Social changes in the community, in spite of galloping industrial and urban expansion, were reluctant, grudging, slow-paced. The Lancastrian, his antecedents deep in colonial history and Pennsylvania-Dutch culture, is not disposed to change; his propensity for order often throttles the dynamics for social and economic justice. The dowager identified herself easily with this powerful, pervasive cultural *status quo*. Naturally, those people least disposed to pioneer felt most comfortable in her company. But Trinity and Lancaster do enjoy rich, vivid heritages.

Historical Setting

Two years before the birth of George Washington and three and one-half decades before Patrick Henry rose boldly in the Virginia House of Burgesses to make his "liberty or death" speech, the Lutheran Church of the Holy Trinity was an established congregation (1730) in the village of Lancaster, then a frontier outpost of the British Empire. A decade before Thomas Jefferson and John Adams struggled with the Declaration of Independence, the nave of Trinity's present church building was dedicated (1766), with the patriarch of Lutheranism in America, Henry Melchior Muhlenberg, officiating. In 1771, four years before the world-shaking skirmishes at Lexington and Concord, Trinity installed the largest organ (Tannenberg) yet built in America. President George Washington was preparing for his second term when Trinity's magnificent tower and steeple, begun in 1785, was completed in 1794. Financed in part by a lottery authorized by the Pennsylvania state legislature, it was not paid for until 1809, the year Mr. Lincoln was born. Still an impressive landmark (195 feet), it was the fixed point for lining up the first railroad in the county. The weathervane, originally set on the spire, employed the first ball bearings manufactured in America.[1]

Trinity parish, rich in religious and secular history, was intimately connected with Henry Melchior Muhlenberg who presided at the cornerstone laying in 1761; his son, Gotthilf Ernst Muhlenberg, who was pastor from 1780-1815, an eminent American botanist, and first president of Franklin and Marshall College; Thomas Wharton, president of the Supreme Executive Council of "revolutionary Pennsylvania"; Thomas Mifflin, Pennsylvania's first governor; and Adam Simon Kuhn, distinguished Revolutionary patriot. Wharton, Mifflin, and Kuhn are buried beneath Trinity's west wall. The congregation, antedating organized Lutheranism in America, was one of eight founding congregations of the first Lutheran synod in the western hemisphere (1748).

The city of Lancaster was laid out in 1730, the year of Trinity's formal organization. A one-time capital of Pennsylvania and one of the nation's nine capitals, the colonial community produced the famous Conestoga (covered) wagon and the Pennsylvania rifle, popularly known on the frontier beyond the Alleghenies as the "Kentucky rifle." The Pennsylvania Dutch were in fact colonial America's best farmers and among its most skilled mechanics and artisans.

---

[1] The historical sources for the sketch on Trinity Church and for the critical evaluations of congregational life are rich and varied. A room-size, fireproof vault houses Trinity's archives: thousands of records, letters, articles, pamphlets, historical sketches, parish periodicals from 1870 to 1964, bulletins from 1920 to 1964, mementos, objects, relics, and an almost unbroken set of parish records (1730-1964). I have also relied on a dozen historical sketches written since the one-hundredth anniversary of the present building and on the research of Mr. George L. Heiges, former president of the Lancaster County Historical Society, and Mr. George W. Leonard, long-time vestryman.

By the close of World War II, "Lancaster had developed an equilibrium in its economy, based on successful agriculture at first, which led to commercial growth, which in turn developed the manufacture of consumer products." [2] This balance between agriculture, commerce, and industry has been maintained. Still the home of Hamilton Watch, Armstrong Cork, Hubley Toys, and RCA, Lancaster, following World War II, became "the home of nationally famous motor boats, electric shavers, electronic equipment, pumps, agricultural machinery, and aluminum products. In the tradition of the Lancaster County farmer, who never depended entirely on one crop for his total income, Lancaster was in no danger of becoming a city dependent upon one or two major industries. With diversity of industry came the promise of future stability." [3] Lancastrians, technologically skilled since the days of the American Revolution, have made their community a significant manufacturer for the affluent society and the missile age. The metropolitan area is also an expanding center of culture and learning with five schools of higher education including Franklin and Marshall College (established in 1787) and the Lancaster Theological Seminary.

So Lancaster and Trinity, born the same year, grew side by side for two and one-quarter centuries. How did the national church and metropolitan Lancaster view the dowager in 1952? How did she see herself? And which images reflected reality?

The Five Faces of Trinity

The image of the congregation in the synod of which it was a member, and which it had helped to create, was lackluster. The

[2] Frederick S. Klein, *Lancaster County Since 1841* (Rev. ed.; Lancaster, Pennsylvania: The Intelligencer Printing Co., 1955), p. 204. Dr. Klein is professor of history at Franklin and Marshall College in Lancaster.

[3] *Ibid.*, p. 218.

28

synod recognized Trinity's place in Lutheran church history but expected little from it in the way of cooperation and generous support. A half-dozen church leaders implied or stated that Trinity's future was in the nineteenth century, that its set ways were beyond change, that the old-line members acted as though they had created their ancestors instead of its being the other way round. Trinity's image in the church-at-large was disheartening to those who see the church as mission.

Trinity's image in the community was equally disturbing. Lancaster, its roots deep in colonial society, is historically self-conscious. The bulk of the homogeneous, old-line population, whether well-heeled graduates of the best schools and prestigious universities or the moderately well-to-do, often congratulating themselves on their ancestors and their ancestors on their thrift, looked on Trinity Church as their very own. Like "Old North" in Boston, it is a prime landmark and was known throughout the area as "Old Trinity." A half decade slipped by before the local people called the church by its proper name, the Lutheran Church of the Holy Trinity!

Then there was the community's view of the congregation itself: proper, proud, exclusive, a strong bulwark against social change. The congregation had a handful of economically dispossessed persons, but it seemed to be *noblesse oblige*, not Christian concern, which prompted a single parish organization to provide economic help for a half-dozen "personally approved" hardship cases. A two-week vacation church school, conducted annually and open to the downtown community, strengthened, albeit unconsciously, the parish's patronizing attitude toward the dispossessed. The congregation was not involved with persons outside its social caste. And the vestry, a self-perpetuating, homogeneous governing board, brought the image into sharp focus.

But this image of exclusiveness was projected most sharply into the community by the antiquated practice of pew rent! Abolished after World War II, the family pew remained a reality for another decade because the several hundred regular worshipers were "lost" in the eight-hundred-seat sanctuary. People simply continued to occupy the same pews. Heavy attendance has wiped out pew sittings, but the image, like Banquo's ghost, rises occasionally to haunt Trinity's lay evangelists. A few members still tax the ingenuity of the ushers, and some people in the community refuse to surrender their inherited view. For a century and a half the "poor" had been expected to sit in the galleries; and the clergy still meet unchurched persons who have refrained from worshiping at Trinity because they either declined, as some Lancastrians put it, to be "herded into the galleries," or feared they would mistakenly sit in someone's pew and be asked to move. Trinity's image in the community as an historic landmark to be pointed out with pride and a congregation that was a closed corporation pleased some, antagonized others, and alienated many.

What was Trinity's image of itself? Actually, the parish entertained several self-images. The most obvious, cherished by many old guard members, was unmistakable: Trinity deserves recognition in Lancaster and in Lutheran circles. The building is sacred; Muhlenberg's constitution (1769) is sacred; the practices and traditions of the church are superior to those in any other church. Touch nothing, disturb nothing, change nothing. This was not a superficial attitude; it was an ingrained temper of mind. Nevertheless, there were wholesome strands in it. The two-hundred-year-old church, an architectural triumph, had been cared for meticulously across the generations. Muhlenberg's 1769 constitution, amended, did prove to be invaluable. Many of the church practices and traditions were notably dignified and meaningful. The flaw was in the disposition of many to revel in the past, employing the parish resources unimaginatively, inflexibly.

The proposed parish house and the calling of a young minister gave the appearance of imaginative leadership. But with few exceptions the parish leaders assumed that they could settle back, confident that these material and human resources, kept under official surveillance and firmly throttled if need be, would give "Old Trinity" a new lease on life without disturbing the stately dowager too much. Younger vestrymen, and the pastor, too, were amused and irritated by this view; but not even they, the pastor included, were yet aware that the gospel, which always comes with fire, would create severe tension and searing conflict as the prelude to a rebirth of ministry in Trinity parish.

Some vestrymen were aware that the congregation was at low ebb, that urban renewal was lagging, and that Lancaster's postwar suburban growth was bringing new pressures to bear on downtown Trinity. But only a few sensed that the real crisis in Trinity was internal, that radical inner change was necessary if the parish were to rise in power. These were not aware, however, that the congregation had little depth in its understanding of evangelical Christianity; that it was theologically immature, imbued with folk religion, indisposed to free Jesus from the stained glass windows; or that it had little sense of God's call to exercise Christ's ministry in and to the world. The primary need was for the clergy, vestry, and parish to come under the Word of the Lord in judgment and grace so that the Holy Spirit could call, persuade, and enlighten persons, each deciding for himself whether he would take up Christ's ministry. The birth of corporate ministry was the only road to the congregation's recovery of God's mission, its only chance to survive. Trinity had to decide.

If this either/or judgment needed strengthening—and it did—another congregational self-image put steel in it. The bulk of the congregation considered the church's work to be the responsibility of its called and elected leaders. Even so, the members had little interest and less confidence in the congregation's future. This depressing image came into sharp focus when the vestry launched the appeal for $150,000 to be added to several hundred thousand dollars then available for the parish house (the bulk having been received in the early 1930's). This modest appeal was subscribed generously by the vestry, several other families, and a few of the visiting teams in the amount of $80,000—a strong beginning. Then the shock came. The congregation— 95 percent of the communing members—pledged only $36,000 on a proposed $400,000 building! A second appeal gained support primarily from those who had previously contributed generously. The majority of members risked nothing on Trinity's future. The isolation of the congregation from its lay leaders was revealed to be total.

This image of a constituency that simply did not care, a people who had lost heart, a congregation without dynamic concern, was a specter which haunted and confused the early years of our mutual leadership. The majority of the congregation, doubting openly that the parish house would be constructed, had even less confidence that a new Trinity could be born. Each afternoon as I visited in the geographically scattered parish, I became depressingly aware how scattered it was spiritually. By mid-1953 several hundred parishioners had indicated that they were considering transfer of their membership. The older vestrymen expected the pastor to stem the threatened exodus single-handed. Two aging trustees put in bluntly: "We'll build the parish house. You get the people to fill it." Meanwhile, the image of sacred traditions and their stubborn power showed no signs of cracking. Most ventures which promised to be constructive were opposed vigorously and involved the clergy and parish leaders in conflicts which only God could make creative. This was true even on the periphery of parish life. So simple a venture as casting a new masthead for the bulletin, designed to awaken hope, received undue criticism. Nevertheless, this masthead was adopted, a brave declaration of faith in the face of an uncertain future:

Trinity Church is the spiritual heir of two and one-quarter centuries of Christian witness in the oldest inland city in America, Lancaster. Originating a half-century before the Declaration of Independence, the congregation is the oldest in Lancaster and one of the oldest in Pennsylvania. The beautiful sanctuary stands today as one of America's frontline colonial churches, historically and architecturally. Humbly grateful for its distinguished place in American history, Trinity aims to stress Christ's ministry to the contemporary needs of the modern city, his atoning power in this atomic age. Trinity, therefore, is a living church with the clear recollection of God's goodness in yesteryear and the hearty expectation of his great blessings in the present.

In spite of our bold declaration of faith the unexpected image of an indifferent, dispirited congregation, linked with the other two images—the old guard's dictum, "touch nothing, disturb nothing, change nothing" and the congregation's view that the ministry of the Word was the clergy's responsibility—dragged the parish leaders into the Slough of Despond on numerous occasions. We turned to bicarbonate of soda for heartburn, to one another for mutual counsel, and to God for hope.

In the early 1950's Trinity was a parish without a sense of mission: a cadre of people who would stand by "Old Trinity" to the death but who gave every indication of standing by each of its confining traditions just as long, a vestry isolated from the bulk of the congregation, a financial appeal which had won no wide support, hundreds of members who were looking to other parishes or simply looking on, and clergy who had little or no experience in meeting pressing practical problems like these. There were the abrasive problems inherent in demolishing an old building; relocating the church school, organizations, offices; constructing and furnishing a new parish house; enlisting a staff; a nonworshiping congregation; a faltering church school; an unrealistic current budget; a deep antipathy toward benevolence. These realities focused our attention on deeper questions. Should a professional fund raiser be employed to gather up the pieces of the disastrous financial appeal? Should the building program be deferred? Should the congregation surrender its historic sanctuary in downtown Lancaster and relocate in the suburbs? Should the congregation's indifference to God's mission to persons be addressed "diplomatically" or confronted boldly? Should the Word of God be trimmed to the secular mind in the parish?

It was a particular congregation which provided the cast for the reenactment of that dramatic scene in Ezekiel 37—the dry bones of dead faith confronted by the eternal Word wielded by flesh-and-blood persons. If the images projected by the parish

34

twelve years ago furnished the description of the problem, it was
the biblical image of ministry and the willingness of some to
discern, accept, and orient the congregation's ministry to it
which opened hearts and minds to God's promise of renewal:
"O ye dry bones, hear the word of the Lord."

—————CHAPTER 2—————
ILLUSION AND REALITY

The unexamined life is not worth living.—Socrates
Let a man examine himself.—Paul

Trinity Church was old indeed! Could its dry bones live?
Could this old church discover the secret of being born again?
How is any congregation persuaded to examine itself in the
mirror of Christ, break free from cultural images of ministry,
and learn to experiment and pioneer for Christ's sake? How is
any congregation motivated, trained, and equipped to be a
fighting regiment in the Lord's army, willing to lose its life in
establishing beachheads for his kingdom? If Trinity parish was
to exercise Christ's ministry in and beyond Lancaster, pastors
and laymen would have to wrestle with the question, "Is that

bush which appeared to Moses . . . the bush which burned and was not consumed, a faithful sign?" [1] At the outset it was imperative that we distinguish between illusion and reality in the life of the parish.

Throughout the twentieth century the parish leaders had served "Old Trinity" devotedly. The corporation had been directed competently. The parish machinery functioned smoothly. Two masterful renovations of the sanctuary had been accomplished since 1923, and several hundred thousand dollars had been received from three families for the construction of a new parish house. Across the centuries the gospel had been preached with theological correctness, the sacraments had been administered faithfully, the parishioners had been visited regularly. The parish appeared to be poised to serve God, but where was the congregation's exercise of Christ's ministry? Trinity possessed the gospel, but the gospel did not possess Trinity. This was the reality of our situation.

The judgment of the Spirit was inescapable; the Lord who had not come to be ministered unto but to minister had been domesticated by outworn traditions, a formal possession of the gospel, and sheer religiosity. Rebirth was the only alternative to slow death, and if we took the Lord at his word, only fire and the spirit could effect the miracle. To have adopted a programmatic approach would have been to treat symptoms, not the disease. A rebirth of ministry was the church's primary need. But what kind of ministry was called for?

Conflicting Images of Ministry in Trinity

Multiple images of the ministry flourished in Trinity parish. Some vestrymen expected the clergy to be religious organization

[1] *The Strangeness of the Church*, p. 14.

men, team executives directing programs and managing persons. Older members cherished the Herr Pastor image—a paternalistic figure, artfully benign and seemingly self-effacing but usurping God's rightful place in people's hearts—a minister who dispensed sage advice, visited formally, and appeared each Sunday morning at eleven o'clock with a "Bible sermon." Here and there an enthusiastic parishioner expected his shepherds to "win souls for Christ," by which he meant new members for the institutional church. Parents and church school teachers insisted that the clergy should rebuild the Sunday school, their favorite church activity. Others—impressed by the historic sanctuary, the tradition of excellent music, and the ancient liturgy—viewed the clergy primarily as priests before the altar and officiants at the Communion services, since these were the only occasions other than Christmas and Easter when two thirds of the members attended church.

Meanwhile, the community, entertaining the same welter of images, added several more obvious secular ones: official prayer for civic gatherings, unquestioning "marryin' Sam," unconcerned officiant at any baptism, recreation director, and problem-solving counselor for marriage hassles. Both the congregation and the community expected the clergy to preach, but the popular view of preaching called for comfortable, twenty-minute homilies stylistically prefaced by a "Bible text" and artfully cast to insulate the hearer against the judgment and grace of God.

Initially, Trinity's members were not waiting eagerly for clergy who viewed themselves as servants of the Word. Neither were the parishioners waiting eagerly to take up Christ's ministry. Some were quick to work for the church, and a few pushed forward to win the recognition in the parish which they could not command in the world; but the parishioners were not inclined initially to admit, let alone pay, any cost of discipleship. On the other hand, the clergy soon discovered that the parish situation demanded significant spiritual growth on their part before they could participate creatively in Trinity's rebirth. Pastors and people had to recognize that they were part of the problem. Hendrik Kraemer, describing the depth dimensions of parish renewal, defined our mutual needs at Trinity in 1952.

The issue is not that, if the laity were only given the opportunity and the right to do so, they would come to the rescue of the Church. The issue is that both laity and ministry stand in need of a new vision of the nature and calling of the Church and their *distinctive places* in it, which means conversion and reformation of the whole Church, laity as well as ministry. Renewal is always based on repentance and new commitment and dedication to the fundamental basis of Christian existence, viz. God's craving for the collaboration with Him of His whole Church, in His work of redemption.[2]

In other words, parish renewal based on the repentance and new commitment of clergy and laity requires that both discern, accept, orient to, and project an authentic image of ministry.

The Crucial Need for Authentic Ministry

But what image is authentic? Augustine in the fourth century appears to have directed persons; the parish priest in the fifteenth century appears to have been a mechanical administrant of the seven sacraments; the preacher emerged as the strong figure during the Reformation; the counselor was sought during the age of pietism; the social gospeler was the dramatic figure prior to the First World War. Since World War II another ministerial

[2] Hendrik Kraemer, *A Theology of the Laity* (Philadelphia: The Westminster Press, 1958), p. 95.

image is becoming dominant in parish life, the pastoral director, although older conceptions—the preacher, the teacher, the priest—are still pertinent.[3] If the blind cannot lead the blind, if the bland should not lead the bland, can perplexed clergy enlighten perplexed parishioners?[4] Certainly the clergyman's self-image as a Christian man and as a minister of Christ is crucial.

Forty years ago Walter Lippmann was arguing the importance of "pictures in the mind." It is generally recognized now—psychology and psychiatry having made the point—that everyone carries about with him a gallery of self-images, one of which becomes dominant. Each considers himself "a rebel or a rock of stability, as an inventor or a destroyer, a genius or a nit-wit."[5] The ordained minister, being human, is no exception. His images of person and ministry affect positively and negatively the congregation he serves and the family he calls into being. If the clergyman commits himself to an image of man and an image of ministry fashioned and projected by culture or sect, he may achieve a measure of personal and vocational success; but he will suffer inner deterioration. And under current cultural pressures the parish that he shepherds will settle into institutionalism or seethe with tension without healing. His last estate will be worse than the first, and likely, his family will be maimed.

Pastors and laymen must come before the tribunal of biblical evidence and, wrestling with that evidence, allow the Holy Spirit to fashion an authentic image of ministry for them. The Word of God in its healing and offense, grace and judgment,

[3] *The Purpose of the Church and Its Ministry*, pp. 79-83. The Trinity report rejects the "pastoral director" in favor of the "shepherd-prophet."

[4] *Ibid.*, pp. 48-58.

[5] Paul S. Minear, *Images of the Church in the New Testament* (Philadelphia: The Westminster Press, 1960), p. 24.

gospel and law is the essential and informing strength and substance of authentic ministry. The particular forms which that ministry employs will vary from culture to culture, and from congregation to congregation, but the transforming power of authentic ministry resides in the Word confronting persons through persons. We concluded, therefore, that the quest must begin not with past or current practices of the "profession" but with the Scriptures' witness to the living Word. The image of ministry evident in prophet and apostle and preeminently incarnate in Jesus had to be discerned and allowed to become the ruling image of Trinity's ministry. The discernment, acceptance, and projection of that image for pastors and people were essential to Trinity's rebirth. They are equally essential to the continuance of its new life.

Keeping alert to the deceptive trap of biblicism, viewing the Bible as a means rather than an end, and taking Christ as the norm for discerning God's Word to man, we searched the Scriptures, discussing and testing the image of ministry which came into focus. Outlined here, it is described fully and its authenticity is demonstrated in subsequent chapters.

The Biblical Image of Ministry

God feeds and provides for the flock of Israel, appoints men to exercise his ministry, and holds each appointee accountable for the welfare of the persons entrusted to him (II Kings 22:17; Jer. 3:15 and Ezek. 34:2). God chastises careless shepherds for neglecting their flocks and allowing them to be scattered (Jer. 2:8; 23:1-4; 50:6). God rebukes selfish shepherds for using his flock as though persons were given to the undershepherds for exploitation (Ezek. 34:1-10). In the third chapter of Ezekiel the shepherd emerges as God's bold spokesman (or prophet), answerable only to God who sent him. He listens eagerly day by day for God's given Word to undergird, sustain, and comfort (make strong) the people committed to his care. In Second Isaiah (50:4-11) the prophet realizes that he strengthens the flock only insofar as he communicates God's truth to individuals; that the confrontation of persons with that truth is every prophet's appointed task even though it brings the wrath of persons upon him; that the acid test of shepherding is fidelity to God's Word.

Jesus accepted, enlarged, and fulfilled the biblical picture which emerged from Israel's custodianship of God's partial self-disclosure in law and prophets. When he spoke of the hireling who flees the endangered flock and identified himself as the Good Shepherd (John 10:11-16), he was not fashioning a new image; he was orienting to and fulfilling an ancient one. Demonstrating that the prophet is one who speaks for God at all costs, Jesus accepted a collision course with Calvary. Obedient to the end ("My God, why . . . ?") and interceding for man ("Father, forgive them"), he gave his life ("No man takes my life") to pay for every man's rebellion against God. The church's embodiment of this Suffering Servant is authentic ministry. The church exists to minister, not to be ministered to; it exists to expend its "given life" for the sake of the world.

This image was the picture in the minds of the apostles. Peter and John demonstrated and taught that Christ's ministers are called to please God rather than men (Acts 4:8-20). James, abhorring "cheap grace," demonstrated that the good news and ethical instruction are inseparable (James 2 and 5). Paul in the book of Romans propagated the view that the church exists to proclaim and teach as the crucial event in human history Christ crucified, resurrected, and victoriously present. The apostolic witness is unanimous: every Christian, accepting the cost of discipleship, exercises Christ's ministry; the Christian community is fashioned by the Holy Spirit for the single purpose of accomplishing God's mission in the world; every person in the household of faith is set apart and, obedient to Christ, is empowered to witness, render priestly service, and share God's love.

We discovered that this biblical view of ministry does not focus on the shepherd's concern for people but on his fidelity to the Word of God. He is any "new man in Christ" who, knowing that he is cared for by the Shepherd and Bishop of his soul, cares for others from Christ's own love. Authentic ministry is not man-centered; it does not stem from an affable disposition, a good digestive system, or a status position in the church. Neither is it dependent on man's good intentions. Obedience to Christ, the disciplined willingness to wrestle with his demands, is the dynamic for Christian shepherding. The shepherd cares for persons because Christ cares, motivating and equipping him to care. The prophet is also *any* "new man" who, accepting God's absolute authority, is enabled to speak God's truth in love to persons who, like himself, are free to reject both the truth and its bearer. This aspect of authentic ministry came especially hard to clergy and laity alike.

We also discovered that unless the God to whom one witnesses is allowed to authenticate himself in the person of the herald, the communication of Christ is delimited sharply. Contemporary culture's preoccupation with communication, as though it were more a matter of form than of content and personhood, reveals how severely "postmodern man" is alienated from God, himself, and other selves. We struggled in facing the hard reality that, if the ordained or lay minister is captive to this sick culture, he will obscure God's Word in the human activities of preaching, teaching, and witnessing. Parishioners who never read Kierkegaard came to his conclusion: where there is no God, there is no self.[6]

Orienting to the Biblical Image

Discerning this biblical image of ministry, naming it for ourselves (shepherd-prophet), testing it, and proving its authenticity provided the frame of reference for continuing analyses, corrections, or rejections of cultural images and partial biblical images of ministry. The businessmen in the parish eventually recognized that the shepherd-prophet will not prostitute himself to be a religious organization man—a pale copy of the corporation team executive hired to manage an institution. The Holy Spirit through the Word in preaching, teaching, and the sacraments persuaded them that God's ministers—ordained and lay— get messily involved with persons and that his ministers accept persons in their freedom and resist the pressures to manipulate them for the sake of an efficient institution. The vestry eventually recognized that neither clergy nor parishioners are employees subject to the direction of a board of trustees, a foreman, or a corporation vice-president; that members and prospectives are free to accept or reject both the gospel *and* its bearer.

But our declination of completely specialized ministries (appealing to clergy and vestry alike as the parish membership grew and the work expanded) was accomplished reluctantly. It required the confused and confusing years of 1955 to 1957 before we discerned and accepted the truth that completely specialized ministries subtly destroy the ligaments of the church's

[6] See Kierkegaard's *The Sickness Unto Death*, translated by Walter Lowrie (Princeton: Princeton University Press, 1941).

effective ministry. But we perceived finally that partial biblical images—*the* preacher, *the* pastoral counselor, *the* priest, *the* teacher—fragment the church's ministry because these images, however convenient, inevitably exalt one function of ministry above the others. Specialized ministries also tempt the clergy to use one of these "holy activities" to escape existential encounters with persons. Further, they allow the clergy to make their specialty a religious status symbol—the *counselor*, the *preacher*, the *administrator*. For example, the *counselor* can become a little tin god; the *preacher* can loom so large that he stands between the congregation and their Bible. These extended critical studies and often heated discussions also prompted us to recognize that the laity can escape God through "church work." Laymen may use committee assignments, evangelistic activities, choir service, and parish offices to hide their persons from other persons and from the righteous person of God. Parish renewal, we concluded, would not happen at Trinity if the clergy were allowed to be "prima donna" specialists or little tin gods and if the laity were allowed to use church work as a cloak of righteousness.

Concerned lest the world, seeking desperately for an authentic word of meaning, hear only the whir of parish machinery and see only a beehive of human activity at Trinity, pastors and people struggled first to distinguish between illusion and reality, to face reality themselves, and thereafter to confront the world with the Word of the Lord. Only if Trinity were converted could this confrontation be possible.

Naturally, there was a season when the parish inquired persistently concerning the place of the ordained minister. If every Christian is called to be a preacher, a teacher, an evangelist, a counselor, what need is there for a professional ministry in the church? Why employ pastors?

The office of preaching (or teaching) and the administration of the sacraments were instituted by God so that his Word might go out to all persons. This ministry of the Word is not an order but an office, a function, a task to be performed. As a means of grace it belongs to the whole church, the community of believers, the people of God, with each believer called to bear witness to his faith and God's Word. This is the priesthood of believers. But a specially trained leadership is necessary. Otherwise, sectarianism results and the ordained ministry—especially called and trained—blurs into the priesthood of believers. Martin Luther phrased it tersely: "We are all priests, but we are not all clergymen." Karl Barth's lifelong colleague Eduard Thurneysen, a parish pastor, puts it this way: "It is the minister before others who has the credentials for pastoral care in that he is ordained and chosen as the shepherd of the congregation." [7] The responsibility for exercising Christ's ministry begins with the ordained clergy; it remains their primary responsibility. But it does not end with them. Christ's ministry is corporate. The congregation, God's royal priesthood of believers, exists to exercise his ministry.

In due time, Trinity's laity recognized that it is a perversion of the concept of the priesthood of believers to allow Christ's ministry to rest wholly on the ordained minister and a few parish leaders. Trinity's clergy learned that it is an equally unrealistic reading of that concept to assume that the laity are waiting eagerly in the wings to witness and render priestly service. They need to be motivated, enlightened, equipped, and encouraged from the resources of God's Word (I Pet. 5:1-4). They

[7] Eduard Thurneysen, *A Theology of Pastoral Care* (Richmond: John Knox Press, 1962), p. 235.

need a script, a producer, a prompter, a "lead actor." Shepherding is preeminently, but not exclusively, the ordained minister's task. All are intended to be priests; not all are intended to be clergymen.

The sensitive observer of human nature and the Spirit-directed student of Scripture will understand that this biblical image of ministry emerged unevenly, messily at times. Subsequent chapters make it clear that parish renewal did not develop in an orderly fashion. Segments of the congregation responded with different levels of understanding and emotion. Some persons made one advance only to experience new offense and fall back two steps before they could consolidate gains and begin again. Here and there minds closed, and hearts hardened. But in that mysterious range where the Spirit calls, persuades, and enlightens, many persons in their freedom decided to learn of Christ, accepted his promises, practiced obedience to his demands, and began to exercise his ministry. How that happened is the theme of subsequent chapters.

CHAPTER 3

CONFRONTATION AND RESPONSE

I urge you then to see that your "flock of God" is properly fed and cared for. Accept the responsibility of looking after them. . . . You should aim not at being "little tin gods" but as examples of Christian living in the eyes of the flock committed to your charge.
—I PETER 5:2-4a (PHILLIPS)

Trinity's clerical and lay leaders, accepting the biblical image of ministry, grew in the conviction that the renewal of their parish hinged on two fundamental issues. The primary issue was whether the parish leadership would accept the authority of God or of man. The second issue was whether the laity could be enlisted and trained as soldiers of the Cross, equipped to proclaim Christ's liberation in enemy territory. But this second issue depended on whether the first decision was properly made.

Only if Trinity parish were truly confronted with the demands and promises of Christ would some persons be motivated and equipped to proclaim his sweeping victory. That meant that the parish leaders—and especially the clergy—had to accept the authority of God and to mediate it through a ministry faithful to his Word. Otherwise, the parish, clinging to its human and cultural traditions, would abort God's power to transform passive members into active witnesses.

Tactics

What tactics, we asked, would accomplish this at Trinity? Certainly the personnel and equipment were at hand. The magnificent sanctuary and projected parish house promised to be strong pieces of field equipment at the center of urban, industrial Lancaster. And there were a thousand potential soldiers on the reserve list, three hundred of whom attended "training sessions" every Sunday morning at eleven o'clock. But how could we get the three hundred off the Sunday morning drill field and into battle on weekdays? How could we persuade the other seven hundred to accept basic training?

A few parish leaders believed sincerely that the equipment and fresh leadership would provide the breakthrough. Some were convinced that our major energies should be directed toward the children and youth. Others called for a major emphasis on evangelism and stewardship. A few saw the need for counseling. Some were enamored of the "small group" approach. Rarely did anyone suggest that preaching could be significant. But as we discerned the biblical image of ministry more clearly, we concluded that God's tactics call for *any* activity in which persons confront persons in their freedom with the Word; that people are motivated and empowered to witness and exercise priestly service by the Holy Spirit working through the Word communicated by persons.

Preaching, teaching, the administration of the sacraments, counseling, visitation, pastoral conversation, "encounter" groups, Bible study groups, youth meetings, catechetical classes are some of the human activities which were employed at Trinity. To assign priority to any one of them would be to report inaccurately. The key to parish renewal does not lie in any single function of ministry. The apostles did not cease to *preach and teach* Christ daily in many ways, in many places. We took this to be the tactics for parish renewal. Certainly we did not assume that preaching, independent of other functions of ministry, could motivate and equip members to witness and render priestly service. But reminding ourselves daily that "Jesus came preaching," we did discover that it is not the ineffectual activity which some contemporary critics consider it to be. However, the critics were right in this: parishes which are mired in religiosity and preoccupied with their institutional life are heavily insulated against the demands and promises of God. This was true of "Old Trinity."

The parish exhibited a complexly stubborn resistance to the Word of God in preaching and teaching—a resistance compounded of traditions grown cold, loose ties to the church as an institution, and a decidedly secular mind. Behind this easily recognized recalcitrance in the parish was a more complex resistance which rooted in that brand of religiosity which treats Jesus with respect but avoids personal involvement with him, venerates the Bible but declines to examine and accept its witness to the Word, and regards the church as a christening, marrying, burying society. This human pietism, like pharisaism in Jesus' day and "works righteousness" in the Middle Ages, acknowledges God while subtly disavowing his will and presuming on his love. At Trinity it cheapened divine grace, robbed the gospel of ethical instruction, and made the word "evangelical" only a piece in the corporate name of the congregation.

When concrete identification of this pietism was made from Trinity's pulpit, the parish reacted. Some were infuriated; others were entertained; a few were set to hard thinking. Because it is the genius of the gospel to expose human piety as a deadly enemy of true Christianity and because persons whose security is not rooted in God are defensive, antagonism and hostility raced through the parish. No mighty army of liberation rose from Trinity's ranks during those early years of gospel preaching and evangelical teaching. But there was response—negative and positive.

During that first confused year we asked ourselves and one another: Will Trinity listen to the Word, let alone obey it? Until the parish heeds God, how can it expect to challenge, much less persuade, the world? Could this parish be converted? And if it were converted, could the clergy and lay leaders really expect the Christian gospel to compete with the other "gospels" clamoring everywhere to be heard? We appreciated the fact that these questions were not new, but we also reminded ourselves that communicating the good news had become increasingly difficult since the turn of the century because the educated world suspects, and in some quarters is convinced, that the Christian message is outworn and obsolete.[1]

[1] Pertinent books on this idea are the following: R. L. Bruckberger, *The Image of America* (New York: The Viking Press, 1959); Emil Brunner, *Christianity and Civilisation* (2 vols.; New York: Charles Scribner's Sons, 1949), II; Herbert Butterfield, *Christianity and History* (New York: Charles Scribner's Sons, 1950); George A. Buttrick, *Jesus Came Preaching* (New York: Charles Scribner's Sons, 1931); C. H. Dodd, *The Apostolic Preaching and Its Development* (New York: Harper &

Facing these cultural realities first in the vestry, the parish
leaders proceeded to discuss them throughout the parish. These
dialogues and group discussions convinced us that the "platform"
pulpit is dead and that contemporary preaching, if it is to be
effective, must be a vehicle for God's Word, culturally relevant,
theologically oriented, and intensely pastoral. It became apparent to us that the cultural climate in which Robertson and
Chalmers, Parker and Beecher had preached so relevantly was
radically different from the cultural climate in which today's
Christians proclaim the good news. We decided that neither
clergy nor laity could preach effectively if they ignored these
awesome cultural problems, accommodated the gospel to a
society, or disdained biblical and theological study.

It became increasingly plain to us that whatever new life
might spring up in Trinity parish would come not primarily
through the human resources of eloquence or style or hard work
but by the Holy Spirit. Confidence in the promises of Christ and
obedience to his demands constitute the indispensable condition
for persuasive gospel preaching. Slowly, the parish perceived
that this kind of preaching is the responsibility of the whole
church; that committed Christians are constrained by Christ's
love to make him known. The mode and style of witness vary
from this person to that, but where people are alert, responsive,
and faithful to the Word, the best of all possible news—"the

Row, 1936); Herbert H. Farmer, *God and Men* (Apex ed.; Nashville: Abingdon
Press, 1947); R. H. Gabriel, *The Course of American Democratic Thought* (2nd ed.;
New York: Ronald Press, 1956); Will Herberg, *Catholic—Protestant—Jew* (Garden
City: Doubleday & Company, 1955); D. T. Niles, *The Preacher's Task and the
Stone of Stumbling* (New York: Harper & Row, 1958); H. Richard Niebuhr, *Christ
and Culture* (New York: Harper & Brothers, 1951; Torchbooks ed.; New York:
Harper & Row, 1956); Paul Scherer, *For We Have This Treasure* (New York:
Harper & Brothers, 1944).

kingdom of God is at hand"—is heralded. Consequently, some
people come forward asking for citizenship in that kingdom.

Pulpit and Pew

Looking back, one can see how certain sermons conceived in this
context and dealing with specific problems in Trinity, Lancaster,
and on the national scene contributed to the breakthrough in
fashioning authentic ministry in Trinity. Part of the pietistic
heritage described above is a retreat from the problems and opportunities of a secularized and urban society in the name of
"religion." If Trinity was to exercise a relevant ministry in a
modern community like Lancaster—urban, affluent, socially
stratified, bearing the scars of deep social injustice—all had to
learn how the Christian faith must drive a man and a congregation into the swirling struggles of the modern world even as it
provides there a firm footing on which to stand and do battle
for the Lord. An early sermon—discussed with several members
during its preparation—was titled "Christian Citizenship in a
Free Society." It began:

Among my minor delights in this abundant life are the Whitney
Darrow drawings which appear in *The New Yorker*, lampooning much
that needs to be punctured. Several years ago a drawing appeared which
has become my favorite. It depicted two clergymen, one young and the
other older, conversing in a richly appointed study. The stabbing
caption read: "Meadows, if you want to get on in the church as I have
done, there are two subjects never to speak on. One is religion; the
other is politics!"

The first point was that the new man in Christ is constrained
by the gospel to bring his Christian insights and judgments to
bear on the body politic so as to create a better society for the

sake of the kingdom of God. Second, he is not hesitant to draw on revelation *and* enlightened reason in judging political philosophies and issues and in seeking wisdom to guide his own political thinking and conduct. Third, the new man in Christ brings light rather than heat to political discussions and campaigns. Finally, he does not equate the interests of his national state with those of the kingdom of God or confuse his loyalties.

Response was immediate. A few persons were captivated; the majority were not. They objected to this sort of preaching: "too personal," "too specific," "not biblical." Some were convinced that the pastor's theological education had set him on the wrong track. Others felt that the trouble lay with the pulpit committee and vestry for having called a "young pastor" to lead "Old Trinity." A few suggested that the pastor had not been called to preach at all! A particularly respected member, a one-time community leader, wrote scathingly in response to the sermon:

Keep politics out of the pulpit. Sermons are expected to help us in our spiritual life. . . . The implication that there are deep faults in the life of this community is not sound. With others, I was working to make this a good community before you entered first grade. . . . Lancaster is an ideal place for anyone to live. . . . Count your blessings and stick to your calling.

The Word stirs some people to negative response; it persuades and heartens others. A tradesman in the congregation was captivated by the sermon. "The church can help me to understand present-day problems and what God expects people like me to do." He began to attend the worship services regularly. During the last decade he has served on the Seventy, as an undershepherd, and as a vestryman. People *do* respond to God's demands and promises set forth in preaching—some with startling quickness.

As sermons became more specific, pointing to dark corners not only in the nation but in Lancaster as well, reaction became more widespread, heated, articulate. The minister was "desecrating the pulpit"; he, of all people, should know that "church is not the place to discuss social and political issues." But the trickle of positive response did not stop. One member, active in community and state affairs, went out of her way to encourage and support the new preaching in Trinity. A few parish leaders began to appreciate and discuss how the Christian who is criticized because he concretely witnesses to the gospel should rejoice to find that the gospel is bringing the fire Jesus said it would bring. The reaction of people who stare coldly at the pastor as they pass by him on their way out of church is to be preferred to the perennial glad hands that indicate the sermon has stirred no one that day, whether for or against Christ. Wherever parishioners begin to react, they are listening; some are thinking. Eventually a goodly number are persuaded. This is how one family remembers the power of God touching them:

Rebellion, indignation, incredulity—these were our initial reactions to the new ministry in our "Old Trinity." Having joined there in our youth—married there—we resented being jolted out of the comfortable complacency of sporadic church attendance, a minimum giving habit, and spectatorism; we had never spoken for Christ to anyone. From the plateau of a happy marriage, we looked upon our religion as an appendage rather than supportive and something to be shared. . . .
Once we dropped the barriers against the changing ministry in our church, our capitulation was complete. . . . So vitalized was the growing congregation that to share in any worship service and the teaching groups was to experience truth with fellowship, the wellsprings from

which we draw strength and guidance to be ministers of God. . . . So real did our commitment become that, upon transfer to another city on the eastern coast, we hastened to find a new church home and are now sharing in its ministry.

When Christ said, "Follow me!" he indicated that movement is forward, into the world and on to the Cross. That was the only direction for Trinity parish. The little band who believed this was growing, but that growth was maddeningly slow. Continuing dialogues with parishioners and rugged give-and-take debates in the vestry made it clear that, since large segments of the parish were still reluctant to change and to go forward with Christ, perhaps a concerted effort to present biblical correctives for their distorted images of Jesus would turn the tide. "Was Jesus Meek and Mild?" asked one sermon. It considered the vibrant humanity of the Nazarene as pointedly as imagination disciplined by the Gospel portraits would allow. It pleaded with the parish to lay aside its flabby, delicately colored pictures of Jesus and to recognize this robust man whose decisiveness in handling God's truth was so clear-cut that he antagonized religious people and political leaders to the point where they had to kill him in the hope of silencing him. The preacher pleaded, "Behold the man," recognize, and accept him as the norm and source of true humanity and authentic ministry.

That sermon—and others like it—awakened the interest of a rising young businessman who had announced earlier that his family was considering a transfer of membership "because Trinity is dead." Demonstrating his new response to Christ's ministry through Trinity, he accepted a "call" to serve as a lay evangelist. Next, he taught in the church school. Today he serves on the official board. But that kind of response was not widespread during our first years at Trinity. Many members remained critical of the preacher for mixing religion and politics, for criticizing their faith, for presenting what they considered to be offensive pictures of Jesus. The preacher should give Bible sermons to comfort people. He should stop attacking their cherished inherited image of gentle Jesus. When the preacher responded privately and publicly that his preaching was true to the biblical witness and that this ministry of the Word *is* comforting (strengthening), some older members replied irrelevantly that he was "biting the hand that fed him."

But members *were* listening and thinking. Some were inquiring into the faith and conversing with the clergy and with one another about the church's ministry. A few were witnessing in the parish and in unexpected corners of the community. This vital stirring in the congregation received support not only through pastoral conversations and through the radical reorientation of the church school but also in the presence of the worshiping congregation. Since most of the members needed to get a biblical view of God, man, the church, ministry, and the world, a series of sermons was fashioned to give the congregation the theological reasons for the new emphases in preaching and teaching, and the practical reasons for fashioning teaching opportunities outside the church school hour and establishing worship services on weekdays.

The initial thrust in this congregation-wide addressment was a sermon titled "Freeing Jonah from the Whale." Announced several weeks in advance, the sermon was discussed fully with several vestrymen and a dozen church school teachers during its preparation so that they could magnify its teaching impact. It dealt first with the form of the book (drama). Next, it pointed to the Scriptures' witness to the living Word through myth, legend, drama, prophets, apostles, and preeminently in Jesus Christ. Finally, recounting the intriguing story of God's reluctant prophet, Jonah, the evangelical message of the book (the Word) was underscored with specific reference to Trinity's limited involvement in and with the community of Lancaster.

This forthright effort to interpret Scripture in the light of Christ and to apply his message concretely to church and community brought the charge from some members that the pulpit was undermining the Bible. The critics—aware that lay teaching in the church school was being oriented to this view of the Scriptures—charged that "Trinity Bible School" was being destroyed. At this juncture the vestry and church school leaders, as well as their clergy, came under attack. Admitting finally that the sectarian mind, as well as the secular mind, was rooted deeply in Trinity parish—in spite of the congregation's formal adherence to confessional theology—the situation was confronted publicly. What we had discussed in the vestry was now discussed in the presence of the whole congregation. This campaign centered in an extended series of biblical-doctrinal teaching sermons on "The Bible and the Word of God": "Creation" (the Word was with God); "Turning Aside to See" (the meaning of the burning bush); the "calls" of Isaiah, Jeremiah, Amos, Hosea, and Paul; "The Incarnation," "The Resurrection," "Conversion," "The Priesthood of Believers," "Prayer and the New Sciences," "The Kingdom of God," and "Christ's Second Coming."

The specific objectives—coordinated with the new thrusts in the church school and the monthly adult Bible study group— were these: persuade the laity to surrender their disposition to treat the Bible as an object of faith and to view it as an understandable witness to God's activity in human history;

persuade the laity to use the Bible as a channel of God's grace for them, *now*; persuade the laity that the biblical doctrine of the Word is an indispensable *tool* for understanding the Scriptures' witness to the living God.

The immediate effect of that series of sermons was increased reaction in the congregation. What happened, some asked plaintively, to the "sweet hour of prayer" when prayer was presented in the light of the new physics and the new sciences of personality? If the priesthood of believers is the redeemed *and* redeeming society—called to costly service and bold witness to the truth—what is left for the preacher to do? In presenting stewardship as something other than a device for getting dollars to maintain an institution—proclaiming that God holds each Christian accountable for his stewardship of the gospel—the people said that the preacher and vestry were judging their lives harshly and unwarrantedly. Segments of "Old Trinity" were not only intensely critical of their clergy but also of their lay leaders for pressing them on "private, personal matters" of the faith. After all, they insisted, "Religion is a man's own business!"

Casual members, gleeful in their mistaken notion that the old guard was being "told off," were reminded plainly that the old guard provided Trinity's only base of operations; that they, like the old guard, were equally under God's judgment and in need of his grace. Miffed, they accused the clergy of being "captive to the vestry." Actually, most vestrymen were among the first at Trinity to discern and support a ministry informed along biblical lines. They not only supported their ordained leadership but enlightened and strengthened it. Parish renewal at Trinity began with the clergy, vestry, and other lay leaders; it did not end there. Signs of new life were unmistakably appearing in historic Trinity. The stately dowager was displaying an un-suspected vigor!

Persons and families were discussing the content and implications of the sermons not only at home but also at work, over bridge tables, at country clubs, in service clubs, at school, on college campuses, at cocktail parties, and in taverns. Equally significant was the rising tide of dialogue between pew and pulpit. Prompted by these dialogues, the clergy selected and shared a wide range of theological and biblical works. The resources of the parish library were developed partly in response to inquiries. Some persons were also guided to the theological seminary library where the staff were willing counselors. A few inquirers, judged able to serve responsibly as they learned, were invited to teach and evangelize in the parish. All inquirers were encouraged and helped to pursue their biblical studies and to foster theological readings and discussions in their homes and among their friends. This running dialogue between pulpit and pew eventually created the stated monthly opportunity for it— "Coffee and Conversation with the Clergy." The dialogues also enriched the people of God by correcting their ordained ministers at various points and challenging them to preach more relevantly. Mimeographed and printed sermons were read and reread, used in discussion groups, and distributed widely by the parishioners. A teen-ager reported that a mimeographed sermon, "God and the Super-Patriots," was the basis for a discussion in a high school class. The memorial sermon for the late President John F. Kennedy found its way into a junior high school. A sermon on marriage was circulated widely in college circles. Ten thousand copies of "God and the Organization Man" were distributed by Trinity members.

The slow but steady growth of the worshiping congregation—

a vigorous witness in any community, the rising tide of dialogue and encounter, the laity's sharing of printed sermons in and beyond the community, and the mounting corps of lay preachers not only attracted new worshipers but also opened doors in business groups, literary and cultural clubs, P.T.A.'s, service clubs, colleges, and the local theological seminary and interdenominational groups for an ever-widening proclamation of the Word. Trinity Church was getting into the world. More than other sermon-encounters for the parish and community in those early years, the one on "McCarthyism" is imprinted on our congregational memory as decisive for Sunday morning preaching by the clergy and for weekday proclamation by lay members.

On a score of occasions pointed observations had been made concerning that virus in the body politic. Suddenly in 1954 this no longer seemed to be adequate. Senator Joseph McCarthy was scheduled to appear in Lancaster to address the Lancaster Manufacturers' Association. Some weeks prior to his coming a series of three sermons was announced on first the philosophical-practical nature of communism, then how the "guilt by association" concept obscured "due process of law" and human freedom, and finally the need for a voluntary revolution in the life of the saints.

Promptly two vestrymen whose friendship and counsel had especially supported Trinity's new ministry sought to alter this announced series. They argued that so controversial an issue should not be taken into Trinity's pulpit, particularly with the senator coming to the city. Their logic was sobering: "The day will come when you can speak on controversial issues. We shall welcome that day, but it has not arrived. If you preach on the issue presently, you will disrupt—possibly split—the congregation." Because these vestrymen were honestly concerned for the congregation's welfare, devoted much time to its work, and also abhorred McCarthyism, I consented to reconsider. Would the proposed series really embroil the congregation in bitter controversy? Would it split the congregation? The situation *was* potentially explosive. That was fat, affluent, complacent 1954— a bad year for prophets! On the other hand, should fear muffle the church's judgment on guilt by association tactics? Was God's clear Word to be denied because some feared that the institutional church could not stand the strain? The preacher's conscience fell captive to the Word of God; he was constrained to preach as announced.

On that particular Sunday in 1954 when McCarthyism was exposed to God's Word, the church was filled, the only time in those days other than Palm Sunday and Easter. Perhaps a hundred business and professional people from other churches, several responsible political leaders, and three hundred or so members who rarely had heard any sermons in Trinity except the meditations at the Communion services were present among the regular worshipers that day. The sermon, delivered in a highly charged emotional atmosphere, was pointed, but carefully documented.

Some visitors were incensed. They said so at the door quite unkindly. The majority of Trinity's congregation, however, departed without comment. Over a hundred letters and phone calls during the next week were evenly divided. The anonymous attacks were harsh, occasionally vicious: "meddling preacher," "Roosevelt lover," "enemy of America." Four times the preacher was identified as "the anti-Christ"! Many signed letters and self-identified callers expressed appreciation and support. The two vestrymen who had sought to dissuade their pastor from preaching on the issue advised him that same morning that a

Christian witness had been made and that they would support that witness. Another vestryman, having endorsed the series from the outset, called it into print and distributed it widely. Harsh criticism came from one segment of the parish, but scores of laymen shared that sermon throughout the community. The decision to bring God's Word to bear on McCarthyism in those frenzied days was one of the more significant specific decisions at Trinity in demonstrating the prophetic utility inherent in gospel preaching.

Thereafter, laymen as well as clergy exploited that dramatic breakthrough. God's Word was proclaimed formally and informally to social man on many fronts by many members. Lancaster's ghettoed Negroes, fair employment practices, open housing, urban renewal, the "organization man," American-Russian relations, nuclear testing, mental health, teen-age sex education, marriage and family, the super-patriots, the 1960 and 1964 presidential elections, civil rights, the acceptance of the Russian Orthodox Church by the World Council of Churches were a few of the political, social, and ecumenical issues hailed before the tribunal of biblical evidence. Trinity Church began to accept its Christian responsibility to examine man and society in the light of God's Word. Learning first that Christianity does not provide pat answers for pressing political problems, or solutions for complex social issues, the parish discovered that Christianity does provide the most relevant frame of reference and the best resources for tackling those problems and issues constructively.

A Rising Corps of Lay Preachers

"So mightily grew the word of God and prevailed" (Acts 19: 20). This is the continuing story of the preaching-teaching ministry in Trinity. The full-time lay assistant and several lay leaders in the parish occupy the pulpit occasionally and preach regularly throughout the community. The minister of music and the office secretaries are also effective lay preachers. And hundreds of members preach and teach Christ spontaneously to one, three, or six persons. Several of these lay preachers will be identified readily by many Lancastrians.

A tradesman, proprietor of a widely frequented shop, preaches daily, unashamedly, effectively. Hundreds of Lancastrians from all walks of life have been exposed to his preaching. Doctrinal, evangelical, and culturally relevant, his lay witness has prompted scores of persons to contact the clergy directly. It has been the means of bringing persons into membership in Trinity Church. It has challenged, encouraged, and strengthened laymen in other churches.

A young factory worker teaches evangelical Christianity during his lunch hour to a number of co-workers—some worldly, others moralistic. He has the satisfaction of knowing that several of them are more knowledgeable in the faith and that several have come into the church through his lay preaching-teaching.

A commercial artist and his wife herald the Word on scores of visits with parishioners and prospectives in the community. Both search the Scriptures, pursue doctrinal studies, and engage their clergy and fellow parishioners in theological discussions. Reared in a legalistic background, they are especially eager in testifying to the liberty of the Christian man. They also participate in a community-wide Christian "encounter" group, enriching and extending their witness to God's re-creative purpose and man's "dreadful freedom."

Although some "organization men" in Trinity have declined to take seriously the God who fashions authentic persons and builds true community, others are striving to obey him. Two in particular are able lay preachers—evangelically sharp, theologically substantial, culturally relevant. They can count a score of new members in Trinity who responded to Christ's appeal through them. Presently, one is seeking to discover whether his part-time witness is enough to satisfy God's persistent claim on his person.

A young engineer and his talented wife—both active in the theater—proclaim the Word in circles ordinarily beyond the reach of their ordained clergy. Both are converts to evangelical Christianity in adult life. Their weekly inquiries into sermons helped to produce the encounter group—"Coffee and Conversation with the Clergy." Recently, the young man accepted responsibility for organizing and leading a religious drama group in Trinity. Under his leadership periodic discussions on contemporary plays and novels are conducted. Presently, he is interested in producing *The Sign of Jonah,* another form of effective preaching.

Another young man, catapulted prematurely into a place of executive leadership, attends every Friday noon and Sunday service in Trinity, evangelizes, and preaches under inner constraint. In a three-page letter evaluating the congregation's impact on his life, he stated that the gospel is equipping him to lead his employees without violating their freedom and enabling him to herald the gospel at social affairs to "many of our friends who go to their churches only when it suits them. . . . They show no theological awareness of why they belong to a particular church or why Christ's church exists in the world. They understand nothing of the layman's ministry. . . . We feel that we must witness."

An exciting counterpart to the evangelist Luke is the competent surgeon who, coming into Trinity through pastoral counseling, demonstrated a maturity which challenged the congregation to call him to its official board, the church school's teaching staff, and the undershepherding program. Our national denomination has also claimed his dedicated talents. He is an effective preacher in many corners of society. During the last six years he has taken extensive notes on the sermons preached in Trinity and has a file almost equal to the clergy's—who dare not rehash a sermon with him in the congregation! From his sermonic library—buttressed by Helmut Thielicke, Reinhold Niebuhr, Tillich, James S. Stewart, and his own biblical studies— he preaches in his home, from Trinity's pulpit, throughout the community, and overseas. Late in 1962 he served a month with a team of medical doctors in Africa. Excerpts from several letters to his wife point up the character of his witness:

December 23 . . . there were four letters waiting for me from you. . . . I enjoyed the *sermon notes* very much [his wife was keeping the file intact].
December 25 . . . I woke up at 6 A.M. . . . I dressed and left the hotel to walk to church at 8 A.M. The sermon consisted of the rector reading a letter from the Bishop of Gibraltar. It was short but did convey a message. *I think I could have preached too.*

Another effective lay preacher in Trinity is the accountant who witnesses regularly to clients and friends. His forthright preaching humbles and challenges his clergy in their uneven acceptance of the prophet's mantle. Across the decade this layman has gone from strength to strength: church school teacher, undershepherd, vestryman, lay preacher. An exciting steward of the glorious gospel of God, he—as much as any one layman—prodded Trinity's clergy to a more realistic teaching of the Christian stewardship of possessions and talents.

A competent schoolteacher persistently heralds the good news in little gatherings of skeptical intellectuals. This is how she reported one situation:

> I'm kicking myself that I hadn't thought to invite ———— to the sermon before Memorial Day. . . . I told him that I was almost tempted to bring the "shut-in tape" [recorded sermon] for his hearing. Then I proceeded to preach the sermon. . . . I was taken aback when ———— who was listening, too, said, "Who needs the tape?"

So Trinity parish—stirred, aroused, motivated by the Word in preaching and teaching—began to witness, too! These preachers and teachers are students of the Bible, theology, and contemporary culture; they meditate and study and worship. This is why they witness to God's mighty deed in Christ. Demonstrating by word and style of life that the gospel is relevant to contemporary society, they refute Peter Berger's sweeping conclusion that

> the most common delusion . . . is the conviction of ministers that what they preach on Sunday has a direct influence on what their listeners do on Monday. . . . The reality, of course, is that the person listening to the minister in church is a radically different one from the person who makes economic decisions the next day. . . . In this second life of his the church is totally absent.[2]

At Trinity, Christ is freeing members from their dual personalities—Dr. Jekyll on Sunday and Mr. Hyde on the other days of the week. The surgeon whom we presented above interrupted

[2] Peter L. Berger, *The Noise of Solemn Assemblies* (Garden City: Doubleday & Company, 1961), p. 37.

his busy practice in November, 1963, to give another month's service overseas, this time in troubled Viet Nam. Arriving there within hours of the revolution which overthrew the Nhu regime, he was a dramatic reminder to Lancastrians that one's next door neighbor can respond to Christ's call to witness and serve creatively in a world filled with tension, hostility, and conflict. After his first term of service in Algeria the doctor wrote concerning his church's ministry:

As a Christian, I am realizing that any skill that I possess as a surgeon has been received from God so that I can help my neighbor through love. . . . The steady preaching of the Word in confronting fashion each week and in vestry and in counseling has focused this for me.

When a friend asked if I would serve with the emergency MEDICO in Africa, I spontaneously said "yes" without any reservation. I felt that this was God's call to me to help those people in need. The ministry in our church, stressing involvement in all of life, has opened a new world of experience for me, not only in terms of places and people, but inside my person as well.

This is ringing rebuttal to Berger's critique that the church is totally absent in the parishioner's second life! And many others in Trinity have also surrendered their double life. They are a growing band because God's Word is quick and powerful, transforming persons who accept Christ's promises and demands. The widespread judgment that the American parish has lost its place in God's overall strategy to save persons is alien to our experience in Trinity Church.

Trinity's lay preachers cause their clergy to remember Wesley's bold claim: "Give me a hundred preachers who fear nothing but sin, and desire nothing but God, and I care not a straw whether they be clergy or laymen, for such alone will shake the gates of hell and set up the kingdom of heaven on earth." [3] Recalling that those Methodist lay preachers did bring a corner of God's kingdom into eighteenth-century Britain, we are excited over the possibilities of lay witnessing bringing Christ into creative conflict with a religionized culture.

This was the breakthrough at Trinity. But preaching alone did not effect parish renewal. It awakened many to gospel faith and motivated them to witness, but this was not enough. These witnesses had to be equipped for their day-to-day encounters with the world. This is the theme of the next two chapters.

[3] *Letters of John Wesley,* edited by John Telford (8 vols.; London: The Epworth Press, 1931), VI, 272.

----------CHAPTER 4----------
DIALOGUE AND ENCOUNTER

Christendom has done away with Christianity without being quite
aware of it.
                                            —SÖREN KIERKEGAARD

Equipping the Lord's army at Trinity has been exciting and
tedious, satisfying and frustrating—arduous at every turn. It
has required the better part of a decade to get a single regiment
into rugged combat. Part of the parish is still on the drill field.
Some ask for "sick leave" at the first sign of being called to battle
duty. One hundred or so rarely answer the call for reveille. The
hard realities inherent in parish renewal, reported in the preceding chapter, come into sharper focus in this and subsequent
chapters. The stages of development in Trinity's renewal remind
one of the federal government's efforts during the Civil War to
train an effective army. We had our sunny days when the recruits

70

looked good at drill, but faltered badly in battle. We had our Bull Runs when the recruits actually broke rank and fled. We had our Gettysburgs when crucial staying actions were waged. Finally, we got a disciplined, experienced regiment to take the field; and like Grant's army at Richmond, we were *willing* to fight. We would win territory for God's kingdom.

The parish leaders—experiencing the gospel's power in preaching to shatter human piety, penetrate worldliness, and motivate persons to serve in the Lord's army—placed their confidence equally in evangelical teaching to equip these recruits for service in the field. Immediately at hand were several hundred children and adults in the Sunday school. That is where we began.

The Sunday Church School

Trinity Bible School, as it was called, was not equipping persons for effective, sustained, spiritual warfare in the mid-twentieth century. Biblicism, theological naïveté, formal worship services in the departments, and an absolute separation of church and school militated against teaching children and adults to discern the Word in the Scriptures and entrust themselves to it. Only a handful of students—or teachers—could give a reason for their faith. Fewer still were constrained by the gospel to witness in the world. Only a third of the school participated regularly in the church worship services. Many teachers and officers were erratic attenders. Here and there a mature Christian teacher oriented to the biblical image of ministry, and the school's monthly offerings—pitifully spare—were directed to needs outside parochial Trinity. But that was the sum of it.[1]

At our first vestry meeting—where the men pledged gen-

---

[1] Compare the historical sources in Chapter 1, note 1.

erously for the new parish house—two vestrymen took the floor to argue stridently that the church school teachers and officers had not been consulted in planning the proposed parish house. The charge proved to be true! After sharp debate the vestry agreed reluctantly to meet with the church school leaders to revise the plans for the new building. Before that meeting occurred, however, the church school superintendent asked to be relieved of her office in criticism of the vestry's disposition to treat the school as a stepchild. Persuaded to stay on the job, she served competently until 1961 when widening professional responsibilities compelled her resignation.

But the time for change at Trinity was especially hospitable in 1952-53. The vestry, planning the construction of the new parish house, simply could not escape giving concerted attention to its school. Secondary changes were effected rapidly. The worship services in the adult classes and youth departments were eliminated, and fifty-five-minute teaching periods were established; the existing opportunity for teacher training was oriented to biblical studies and confessional theology, and was made a requirement; the establishment of a theological library was authorized; the name of the school was changed from Trinity Bible School to the Sunday Church School, the *congregation's* teaching arm. These were the beginnings, but more fundamental changes were called for.

The vestry and church school association diagnosed and faced up to a teaching situation which had prostituted evangelical teaching by its uncritical acceptance of biblicism and its accommodation to contemporary culture's anti-intellectualism.[2]

[2] Particularly helpful: Ralph D. Heim, *Leading a Sunday Church School* (Philadelphia: Fortress Press, 1950); James D. Smart, *The Teaching Ministry of the Church* (Philadelphia: The Westminster Press, 1954).

Diagnosing our situation, admitting our need to understand the Scriptures' *witness* to the living Word, wrestling with the relationship between revelation and reason, struggling to balance biblical-doctrinal teaching with dialogue in dynamic learning experiences, was the second step. Next, we examined several bustling, well-attended Sunday schools in our three-county "Bible belt." We concluded that parish education, allowed to focus exclusively in the Sunday school, becomes another parish "activity" insulating persons against the demands and promises of God. Expecting no panacea for our teaching situation which was in the doldrums, we rejected promotional schemes and attendance crusades. We agreed that results should be measured in terms of Trinity's fidelity to the Word in teaching. By mid-1954 we were acting on these propositions: (a) content teaching, rooted in biblical and confessional theology, is essential; (b) committed, competent teachers are indispensable; (c) the clergy are called to teach as well as preach; (d) adults and youth must be taught in special settings outside as well as during the church school hour. In 1954 we called an ordained associate to share in Trinity's total ministry.

The need for teacher training was addressed immediately. The local council of churches' leadership school—in those years calling on local college and seminary professors, trained laymen, qualified parish pastors—gained Trinity's vigorous support. Our new parish house at the center of the city housed the interdenominational school. Staff members, lay teachers, and other laymen were encouraged to enroll. Trinity's staff also offered teacher training on departmental lines, by subject, and according to special interests. One six weeks' session introduced sixty-five laymen to Buttrick, A. B. Bruce, and Richard C.

Trench on the parables of Jesus. Another six weeks' session offered "John's Portrait of Jesus"; mimeographed materials compiled from a half-dozen scholarly sources were shared with the participants. Another series dealt with "The Bible and the Word of God."

During the last four years seminars for the church school teachers have been offered on departmental lines. The same source material is used in each seminar, but the emphasis is geared to the teaching needs of each department. One year Gilbert Highet's *The Art of Teaching*, suggested by a parishioner, was the creative resource book which teachers were required to read prior to participating in the seminar.[3] Our experience with the book constrains us to call it a "must" for *all* teachers. Other seminars provided the opportunity for depth studies on "The Prophets," "The Life and Work of Jesus," and "The Pupil." At the close of a recent seminar an executive said, "I really understand now what we mean by the Scriptures testifying to the Word of God." Another teacher quietly stated: "At last the Bible is intelligible to me." But these insights were long in coming. The clergy expended hundreds of hours—literally—in equipping the lay teachers through individual as well as departmental meetings.

When the congregation occupied the new parish house in December, 1954, the parish leaders at least were aware that the new equipment would be a mockery if the quality of teaching in the school was not radically improved. It was mutually agreed, therefore, that all teachers in the school should be challenged to accept a printed call which defined precisely what the church expected of its teachers. The document, reflecting scores

[3] (Vintage Books ed.; New York: Random House, 1954).

of pastoral conversations and sanctioned by the vestry and church school association, was placed before each active teacher and officer. Those who declined to sign it were allowed to withdraw. Since its introduction no one may teach in the church school unless he affirms the call. Enlisting a teaching staff is no longer a perfunctory exercise. It is accepted as a primary responsibility by the clerical *and* lay leaders.

THIS CALL to teach in the —————————— Department of the —————————— Church School of the Lutheran Church of the Holy Trinity is hereby extended to you after careful consideration and earnest prayer.

This call is extended to you in full confidence:

1. That you are committed to the person of Jesus Christ, our Lord.

2. That you share the basic confessional position of the Lutheran Church, as enunciated in the Augsburg Confession and Luther's Small Catechism, copies being attached hereto.

3. That you worship regularly within the fellowship of Trinity Lutheran Church.

4. That you are an increasingly responsible steward of your possessions, either acccepting in reality or as your goal the tithe as the first reasonable step in Christian giving.

5. That you will earnestly consider, against your own background, training, experience, and felt needs, the worth of opportunities offered for further training.

6. That you believe in and act upon the prior call of every Christian to the task of personal evangelism.

7. That you will conscientiously strive to nurture in Christian growth those placed under your care, making use of all resources available and taking as your own the responsibility to hold them by prayer, visitation, and calls.

It is expected that you will pray earnestly as you consider this call, remembering not only that he who teaches is judged with great strictness but also that from those to whom much has been given much is expected.

In Christian Witness Whereto
We Here Affix Our Signatures:

_____

Superintendent

_____

Department Superintendent

Acceptance

Mindful of the sacred trust to those who teach the gospel of Jesus Christ our Lord, and of the joy which comes to those who serve him, I hereby accept THIS CALL extended in the name of the Church School Association of the Lutheran Church of the Holy Trinity,

Lancaster, Pennsylvania, to teach in the _____ Department

of the School or to serve as _____ of the school.

Date _____

Signed _____

Waves of misunderstanding engulfed the parish leaders when they presented and interpreted this call to every teacher and officer in the school. One church school officer, having endorsed the call, turned critical of it when a department superintendent declined huffily to sign it and was advised that his service was terminated: "After all, isn't he getting interested? You'll lose him to the church." Under these pressures a few lay leaders faltered, but most stood firm. The crucial battle was won.

The widespread assumption that good character, personal affability, and casual churchmanship are adequate qualifications for the Christian teacher is an affront to those Christian parents and children who worship, evangelize, and serve. It is a cheap view of God and man which assumes that a disciplined approach to Christian teaching alienates most church members from Christ. Some at Trinity were alienated, but the majority accepted the call as a proper discipline. A lawyer and an executive, invited to teach in the school, were at first reluctant to accept the call. After several counseling sessions they perceived its significance, acknowledged its demands, signed it, and accepted teaching responsibilities. Today both men are able teachers, responsible stewards, and former undershepherds; one is a vestryman. A teaching staff of bland Christians will ruin the finest planned curriculum. Confrontation is the crucial need; persons must decide for Christ before they can teach him persuasively. Diagnosis, discussions, and declared principles are academic exercises apart from confrontation and decision. The call, with its intent and spirit interpreted to each new teacher, has helped in fashioning a consecrated, competent faculty which includes many of the ablest Christian people in Trinity Church —tradesmen, mechanics, doctors, public school teachers, housewives, executives, salesmen. Furthermore, it is significant that *men* teach the pupils in grades four through twelve, ages nine through eighteen.

Across the years participation in the church school, ages one through eighteen, increased threefold; but participation in the adult school did not keep pace. During the first years the clergy and church school superintendents had deliberately given their primary attention to strengthening the faculty and curriculum for the children and youth. By 1956, however, one ordained staff member was devoting a third of his time to the organized classes in the adult school. The fruits did not justify these labors. Accordingly in 1960, the vestry and church school association voted to dissolve the organized adult classes and to adopt the elective system.

Some participants in the adult school were not enthusiastic about this change. Others were eager for it—especially those leaders in the school who complained, and rightly so, that the weight of running the adult classes, as well as teaching responsibilities, fell on the same people. The majority accepted dissolution of the classes and agreed to experiment. The schedule of courses, mailed to every church member, described the two-year teaching thrust.[4]

I. *February 5 to May 28, 1961*

Each of the two courses offered will meet for fifteen sessions.

A. "What Lutherans Believe"—A study of the church's confessional position, using *Luther's Small Catechism* and the *Augsburg Confession* as resources.

B. "The Corinthian Letters"—A study of Paul's two letters to the Corinthian Church with some attention to other letters as time permits.

[4] In addition to the resource books listed in the schedule of courses, others were also used fully or in part by the teachers and some pupils. Examples are the following: D. M. Baillie, *God Was in Christ* (New York: Charles Scribner's Sons, 1948); Roland H. Bainton, *Here I Stand* (Nashville: Abingdon Press, 1950); Oscar Cullmann, *The State in the New Testament* (New York: Charles Scribner's Sons, 1956); Herbert H. Farmer, *God and Men*; Georgia Harkness, *Understanding the Christian Faith* (Nashville: Abingdon Press, 1947); C. S. Lewis, *The Screwtape Letters* (New York: The Macmillan Company, 1961); Ernest F. Scott, *The Purpose of the Gospels* (New York: Charles Scribner's Sons, 1949); James S. Stewart, *A Man in Christ* (New York: Harper & Row, 1935); Daniel Day Williams, *What Present-Day Theologians Are Thinking* (Rev. ed.; New York: Harper & Row, 1959).

II. *June 4 to June 25, 1961 (open forum)*

"A Family Institute"—Man and wife relationships; parent-child relationships; family-community relationships.

III. *July 2 to September 3, 1961*

Single class sessions, Fondersmith Auditorium, 9:45 A.M. (ten lay teachers).

IV. *September 10 to December 31, 1961*

Two courses will meet for fifteen sessions.
A. "How to Read the Bible"—A survey of the "tools" of Bible study, with an application to actual passages of scripture in the later sessions.
B. "The Life and Teaching of Jesus Christ"—James Stewart's remarkable text will be used.

V. *January 7 to May 27, 1962*

Two groups will meet simultaneously, one course continuing for nineteen sessions, and three courses running for six, eight, and five sessions.
A. "The Sermon on the Mount"—A nineteen-session depth study of this first of the five great discourses in Matthew's Gospel.
B. (1) "What's Behind the Liturgy"—A six-week study of the Common Service, Matins, and Vespers.
   (2) "The Life of St. Paul"—An eight-week appraisal of the man who first proclaimed Christ to the western world.
   (3) "Alternative to Futility"—A five-week study of Dr. Trueblood's Christian answer to a confused world.

VI. *June 3 to September 2, 1962*

One course only, Fondersmith Auditorium, 9:45 A.M.
"The Church and Social Responsibility"—Three sessions; an appraisal of the church's role in the face of such social problem areas as race relationships, labor-management disputes, war and peace, etc. *Single class sessions thereafter.*

VII. *September 9 to December 30, 1962*

Two electives for fifteen sessions each.

A. "An Introduction to the Old Testament"—This course will continue for thirty-three sessions through the last Sunday in May, 1963.

B. "The Reformation"—A study of its permanent spiritual contributions.

New students enrolled in the electives immediately, effecting a sharp increase in adult participation during the first year. The eager response of the church school teachers who began to rotate on sabbaticals and attend the electives was gratifying. The parish leaders—encouraged by the congregation's steady growth in worship, evangelism, and stewardship—mistakenly anticipated continuing growth in the adult school. The surge in adult participation was short-lived. Adult attendance settled to the old level within eighteen months. The disposition of some persons to sample an occasional lecture, attending at whim, disturbed the total teaching situation. But the real flaw was this: young families attending the early worship service in strong number (five hundred to six hundred) clamored for fellowship as the necessary context for a "learning experience." One member expressed the thoughts of many like him when he wrote:

I can do without "sweet fellowship," but I cannot manage without some kind of fellowship and encounter. For my money, this was the chief value of the old Family Class. . . . Now there is little opportunity for discussion, for a "meeting between minds," for stating an idea poorly or incorrectly, and realizing this, learning thereby. If the full value of the excellent preaching and teaching is to be realized, each parishioner must stumble through his "homework," somewhere, somehow. Some will accomplish this within the family circle; some only within Trinity circles. Mere receptivity, we have agreed, is meager learning.

Once again, therefore, those who preferred the organized classes and those who were enthusiastic for the electives were consulted, and their representatives convened. Not many, we discovered, wanted to resurrect the "clubby" men's, women's, and family classes weighted with organizational machinery and marred by cliquish tempers of mind. But the participants insisted that fellowship and dialogue, lacking in the elective system, had to be recovered. After six months' study and discussion three age-interest groups were established. It was unanimously agreed that competent lay teachers would be *appointed* (in consultation with the clergy) to present the same prepared course in each of the three age-interest groups during the year, and that the age-interest groups would not be organized, even though each would have a chairman.

This modified venture, initiated in the autumn of 1963, enjoyed the support of both parties and the staff. Biblical-theological content and sound pedagogy were provided through a mutually agreed upon curriculum and teachers chosen for their competence and experience. The program also provided opportunity for persons to establish and nurture Christian friendships and to engage in dialogue and encounter. Twelve able lay teachers served, with none preparing more than four lesson units. During the summer months ten other lay teachers presented a single lesson. This was the curriculum and the number of sessions: "What Happens Through Baptism?"—four; "The Freedom of the Christian Man" (Galatians)—four; "One Man Speaks Out" (Isaiah)—eight; "Getting Acquainted with Great Religious Music"—four; "Christianity and Communism"—

eight; "How to Study the Bible"—four; "Jesus Christ and the World Mission"—four.

But age-interest groups did not prove to be an effective medium for educating adults in Trinity's church school. The older adults missed their stimulating contacts with younger persons. The young and middle-aged members considered the division by age to be artificial. Once again, therefore, the staff and lay leaders in consultation with the teachers and participants modified the teaching form in the adult school. This program—initiated in September, 1964, calling on the existing corps of proved lay teachers and using the splendid material from our new denominational curriculum—was offered to the congregation through this announcement in our parish publication:

ADULT COURSES
Trinity Lutheran Sunday Church School

All adults are invited to meet in a single class in the Fondersmith Auditorium, 9:45 A.M. every Sunday, for a consideration of vital themes from the Old Testament. Currently on sale for individual study coinciding with the courses listed below is a text, *The Mighty Acts of God* by Robert J. Marshall.

GENESIS, IMAGE OF MAN IN A TROUBLED WORLD—September 6-20, three sessions.

An investigation, within the context of modern knowledge, of the biblical narratives of creation and their relevance for modern men and women. Mrs. Ann Musselman teaching.

> September 6—"Man, Made in the Image of God"
> September 13—"Man, the Eternal Rebel"
> September 20—"Man, Sinner and Sufferer"

COFFEE AND CONVERSATION WITH THE CLERGY—September 27

DIALOGUE AND ENCOUNTER

CHOSEN BY GOD—October 4-18, three sessions.

Through the study of important Old Testament persons the method of God's activity in history is revealed and applied to the life of the contemporary Christian. Mr. Wilfred P. Bennett teaching.

October   4—"The People of God," Filmstrip
October 11—"Called to Be Counted"
October 18—"A Contract With God"

COFFEE AND CONVERSATION WITH THE CLERGY—October 25

AMOS AND THE PROPHETIC MIND—November 1-22, four sessions.

The meaning of life is clarified by one of the foremost prophets of the Old Testament when his own life emerges as a living reality. Mr. Merle V. Hoover teaching.

November   1—"What Is a Prophet?"
November   8—"Inspiration and Activity"
November 15—"Prophetic Life and Worship"
November 22—"Judgment, Source of Salvation"

MOTION PICTURE (to be announced)—November 29 [5]

UNCHANGING REALITIES—December 6-20, three sessions.

A consideration of basic biblical themes with contemporary relevance as expounded by Jeremiah, the prophet "most like Jesus." Mrs. Dorothy Bolbach teaching.

December   6—"Choices for Survival"
December 13—"Doubt, Suffering, and Faith"
December 20—"Personal Hope and Individual Responsibility"

COFFEE AND CONVERSATION WITH THE CLERGY—December 27

[5] November 29, 1964, was Advent Sunday; there were four stated services of Holy Communion, one running simultaneously with the church school hour. "Coffee and Conversation with the Clergy" was cancelled on that Sunday.

This new form provides an opportunity for social contacts, biblical-doctrinal teaching, direct questions and open discussion, and a full hour of dialogue monthly with the clergy. Perhaps this venture will attract many new persons into the adult Sunday church school. Meanwhile, the school's several hundred participants do come under God's Word in a competent content teaching situation.

The Sunday church school hour, however, is only one medium among many where the disciples are equipped to be witnesses, teachers, preachers, and counselors. It had been agreed years earlier that the parish must also provide varied teaching situations for adults and teen-agers at times other than the church school hour. The remainder of this chapter reports on several of these special teaching situations.

Teaching Outside the Church School Hour

Trinity Church had required for years that its youth thirteen to fifteen years of age, receive, prior to confirmation in adult church membership, two years of Christian instruction weekly from September to Palm Sunday. At the outset the clergy asked for and the vestry authorized a separate hour for this significant task. The altered approach called for catechetics at five o'clock each Sunday evening, an informal youth supper at six, and two separate youth meetings, according to age, at six thirty. The Family Class from the "old" church school accepted responsibility for serving the suppers; several laymen joined the clergy in shepherding and teaching the youth. Demanding requirements on attendance, homework, and class participation produced tensions in some families; but they also contributed to a wholesome teaching situation. During the decade the total enrollment in the two catechetical classes increased from twenty-one to eighty-three. Attendances at the youth programs climbed from a "baker's dozen" to ten times that number. Presently, 90 percent of the parish youth worship regularly after confirmation; 20 percent tithe; many are eager evangelists; and with few exceptions they come readily for pastoral counseling —premarital, vocational, and personal. The demand for disciplined learning has brought Trinity's youth into the church.

The curriculum for the second-year class calls for a weekly discussion of the sermon, open discussion on the assigned daily Bible readings, observations on pressing sociopolitical issues, and lecture-discussion on weekly assigned homework. During the course, one to three hours is given to these doctrinal-biblical-ethical subjects: The Bible and the Word of God; the person and work of Christ; the nature and purpose of the church; worship; study, prayer, and daily decisions; the Apostles' Creed and the Ten Commandments; the Lord's Prayer; baptism; the Lord's Supper; Christian vocation; dating, courtship, and marriage; personal responsibilities to church, family, employer-employees, community, and nation; evangelism and stewardship; the Christian view of death and resurrection; and the meaning of the rite of confirmation.

God's Word is brought to bear specifically on the students' daily life in a continuing effort to equip them to discern it and use its resources. Frank discussions during class sessions reveal teen-age problems: misconceptions of God; collisions with parents; difficulties in school; confusion over sex, love, and marriage; concern over race relations and social cleavages in Lancaster; confusion in the face of the competing political philosophies in the nation and the world. These open discussions create the dynamic context for teaching the relationship between worship and morality, Bible study and ethical decisions, prayers and plans. They also foster the wholesome interpersonal relationships which open doors for creative counseling.

The formal church service of confirmation provides a meaningful setting for the youth, carefully taught and individually counseled, to make their vows. The impressive confirmation service also persuades many adults to look down the corridors of yesteryear and renew their confirmation vows. Trinity Church seeks to care for its children from infancy through the teens, into courtship and marriage, into a vocation, and thereafter seeks to guide them in bringing a new generation into the church through baptism and continuing instruction in the faith.

Some parents of the catechumens, while supporting the full Sunday evening youth program responsibly, nonetheless kept pointing out that a family's weekly participation for two hours on Sunday morning and another two hours each Sunday evening, coupled with an additional hour or so for transportation, shattered the "family Sunday"! They suggested that catechetical instruction be given during the Sunday morning church school hour. Because the parents were arguing from the position of responsible participation in the church; because the youth program was strong enough to stand alone; because parishioners with children *were* worshiping regularly, giving generously, and evangelizing; and because the catechumens and the confirmands were attending church faithfully, the change—after a decade— was agreed to on a trial basis.

Put into practice, it immediately strengthened teen-age participation in the church school because regular attendance during both years of catechetics is required for confirmation. The Sunday morning pattern was reviewed carefully in the autumn of 1964 when the splendid new curriculum of our denomination was introduced. The clergy and vestry decided that the youth—

worshiping regularly and participating weekly in the youth programs—were equal to "double content" in the seventh and eighth grades. Clergy and laity do the teaching. Strong pastoral ties continue to be forged with the youth.

These two random excerpts from the letters of college students convey the youth's willingness to turn to their church.

We had an exciting "bull session" at the fraternity late Tuesday night. No, "broads" were not the subject—not this time. We got on the "organization man" and had it hot and heavy. . . . I remembered parts of the sermon, "God and the Organization Man," and its arguments made sense to many of the fellows.

——— is pregnant. We've made love several times and want to marry because we love each other. We haven't said a word about ——— condition to anyone. What's our first step? We want to marry, but. . . .

Presently, a full-time lay assistant is responsible for the two weekly youth meetings. The Intermediate League, ages twelve through fourteen, has a supper meeting each Tuesday evening after school; the Senior League, ages fifteen through eighteen, meets on Sunday evenings at seven o'clock. One hundred and sixty teen-agers are enrolled; the average attendance is one hundred and fifteen. Both groups have parties, dances, and social outings. Five years ago a teen-age canteen was initiated under the direction of the present lay director, who was at that time a vestryman and the associate executive director of the local United Community campaign. The canteen, open to all young people in the city and attracting 65 percent of its clientele (10 percent Negro) from the environs of the church, received a Lancaster Community Betterment award in 1961. When local church and community leaders suggested it—the attendance of seven hundred teen-agers overwhelmed Trinity's parish facilities and lay personnel—the canteen was surrendered to wider community sponsorship. Our parish youth continue to have dances, inviting whom they want and directing these smaller affairs.

The heart of the youth program, however, is a teaching fellowship which calls teen-agers to accept Christ's promises and instructs them in his commandments. The Tuesday and Sunday evening meetings center in faith and life studies: (1) the Christian and his vocation, with physicians, lawyers, and businessmen, (parishioners) addressing the youth and answering their questions; (2) Christianity and Communism, God and the "Super-patriots," and other critical sociopolitical issues; (3) Christian doctrine—the Word, the church, Christ, justification, the ministry, the sacraments; (4) Christianity and religious drama; (5) Christian ethics and social living—school, dating, courtship, marriage, alcoholic beverages, status, etc. The youth speak freely and frankly; no question is sidestepped.

One of the far-reaching thrusts of Trinity's youth program is its sponsorship of an annual teen-age forum on dating and courtship. Conceived by the lay youth director, open to all young people and youth leaders in the community, the first forum attracted Trinity's youth and a few guests. The second forum reached several hundred persons beyond the parish. The third overflowed the parish house auditorium—five hundred teen-agers, clergy, teachers, and youth workers attending. The fourth, in 1963, overflowed the auditorium and four other sections of the parish house, with seven hundred youth and their directors attending. The senior pastor, engaged daily in counseling, is invited to make these annual presentations. The most recent forum, which called forward sixty-eight written questions from the youth, received front-page coverage in the local newspapers. One anonymous parent railed: "You people at Trinity are just crazy—You talk sex to kids, love Negroes, and oppose the Holy Bible in the schools." A clerical colleague in the community commented: "Sorry I missed the teen-age forum at Trinity last night. The newspaper report made clear how worthwhile it was. . . . We are planning a forum, too. . . . Trinity's example challenges and encourages us."

The congregation's willingness to meet young people with Christian realism prompts these youth to seek counsel concerning their personal problems. They come expecting acceptance, understanding, and help from the resources of the gospel; but they do not expect to be excused from its demands. This forthright reliance on an evangelical approach to teen-agers, described in Chapter 6, also binds many of their families to the church, and frequently opens vital teaching-counseling opportunities with parents. The basic purpose of Trinity's youth program is to instruct teen-agers in the knowledge of God and to equip them to use the resources of the gospel in daily living.

From the beginning the vestry showed concern for the parish youth. They shared in the planning, endorsed the new programs, provided the necessary funds, chaperoned dances, and accepted even wider responsibilities. One vestryman's notably creative contributions convinced the clergy and congregation that he should be invited to a full-time place on Trinity's staff; he accepted. Responsible for youth work, the senior adults, and parish administration, he also works cooperatively with the staff and vestry in evangelism, stewardship, and parish visitation. His office is *not* primarily administrative; he is a minister of Jesus Christ.

The Adult Bible Study Hour, inaugurated in 1955, provided another special teaching opportunity. Meeting on the first Sunday night of each month for six years, it was discontinued when the electives were inaugurated in the Sunday church school, when Bible study was entrusted to the undershepherds, and when weekly Bible study under the lay assistant's leadership was offered each Friday noon at the parish house. The monthly meetings during those six years called for an hour-and-a-half lecture: historical background, literary character, exegesis, and the Lord's Word to Lancastrians. Open discussion followed each presentation; stated half-hour intervals allowed persons to leave comfortably. The Sunday evening sessions began at six thirty; the last twenty or thirty persons departed at ten thirty! Monthly attendances ranged from seventy-eight to one hundred and eighty-four persons; the average for the six-year period was one hundred and forty-three. Five hundred *different* people participated. Seventy-three individual teaching opportunities emerged. To our knowledge thirty or so families initiated home Bible study. Almost a hundred participants became church school teachers, evangelists, and lay preachers.

A year each was devoted to the study of the following biblical books in this order: Luke, Acts, Matthew, Isaiah, Genesis, and Revelation. Each lecture was introduced and illustrated differently each month by a brief statement on the relationship between the Scriptures and the Word of God. Slowly, imperceptibly at first, the participants began to appreciate that the Scriptures are an uneven collection of human documents written by persons of inspired faith in God, with each document testifying to the God who revealed himself across the centuries in myth, legend, law, prophets, apostles, and preeminently in Jesus Christ. At each session we demonstrated from the Gospels and Epistles how the early church's witness to the Word produced the New Testament. Following these introductory observations, each lecture claimed seventy-five minutes. Promptly at eight o'clock the group turned to questions and open discussion with half-hour breaks until ten thirty.

The year given to studies in the book of Revelation was possibly the most significant—examining Luther's ambivalent attitude toward the Apocalypse of John, presenting the historical setting in which the document was composed, and digging at its imagery. Its central message came into sharp focus: salvation is not only mundane; it is eschatological. The year-long study, with cross-references to the book of Daniel, contributed to the transformation of the sectarian mind in Trinity congregation. That year, more than any other, we learned to read Scripture in the light of Christ, the true norm for discerning God's Word to man in the Scriptures.

The Adult Bible Study Hour contributed greatly to the rebirth of Trinity Church and the strengthening of its new life. Other churchmen have reported in detail on their experiences with Bible study groups; our experiences parallel their enthusiastic testimonies. But the notion that Bible study groups and prayer cells transform the church is foreign to our experience at Trinity. They are one means among many. We also learned that the Bible study group may harden into another parish activity. When we caught the first sign of this happening, we closed the meetings and devised other means for teaching the living Word.

Presently, segments of the parish are engaged in small Bible study groups under lay leadership. It appears that three hundred or so persons, including teen-agers, engage in daily personal Bible study and that family devotions have established a firm beachhead in the parish. Two small prayer groups, spontaneous in origin, meet weekly in the parish house. A handful of men are examining the possibilities of the weekly "prayer breakfast."

Seventy older people meet each Friday in the parish house for Bible study under lay leadership. Ninety lay evangelists also meet periodically for Bible study with an ordained staff member, and a half-dozen cell groups function in the parish without any professional guidance. The formal Adult Bible Hour was one medium among many which fostered these current evidences of spiritual vitality in the congregation.

For half a decade book reviews by the staff, open to the parish and their friends, provided another special teaching arena. Attendances ranged from forty to one hundred and seventy-five persons. Vance Packard's *The Status Seekers,* R. L. Bruckberger's *The Image of America,* Jaroslav Pelikan's *The Riddle of Roman Catholicism,* Dietrich Bonhoeffer's *Prisoner for God* are typical of books which were reviewed. Following each review, discussion over coffee opened the way for exciting dialogue and rugged encounters. Pelikan's book, together with other studies on Roman Catholicism, helped to fashion the congregational temper of mind which made it possible to sponsor a community forum on the 1960 presidential election's religious issue. Early in 1964 Trinity opened its parish house auditorium to and participated in the first Roman-Protestant service in Lancaster County.

The book reviews were undertaken with these stated objectives: introduce parishioners, according to their intellectual curiosity and spiritual readiness, to the enrichment to be gained from reading serious literature; demonstrate the Word's relevance to socioeconomic and political issues; encourage personal encounters through group discussion; and provide opportunities for fashioning Christian friendships. The book reviews, unlike the Bible Study Hour, did not call out a corps of regulars.

Four years ago at the suggestion of interested parishioners, the pattern of formal book reviews was recast. The new pattern, "Books and Coffee," rests on personal invitations issued with the understanding that the participants will first read the book to be discussed. This approach—invitation by preparation— provides more lively dialogue and more meaningful encounters. One year, nine groups, with twenty to twenty-five persons in each, read and discussed Martin Marty's *The New Shape of American Religion*. The laity were quick to grasp the book's thesis, recognizing readily those areas where they had struggled or were struggling. Some, not aware that this report was taking form, suggested that it should be made. Five participants from the groups which met that year read and criticized the first draft of this manuscript.

Another year seven groups, each limited from fifteen to twenty persons, tackled Seward Hiltner's *Self-Understanding*.[6] The venture was strikingly creative. Two sessions became in fact group therapy, opening the door to thirteen new pastoral counseling situations. Hiltner's book was used again the following year with equally creative results. Half the participants in each group were former counselees (the best leaven!), many of whom had read the book years before on loan from the clergy's library. But all participants had immediate access to the dozen paperback copies in the parish library.

These intimate groups for "Books and Coffee" are designed to bring together persons from different social and cultural backgrounds. Conducted in the parish social lounge or in the homes of the clergy, the meetings open opportunities for establishing meaningful friendships through Christian encounter. We discovered that when these small groups of persons from

---

[6] Several hundred parishioners have profitably used this book, recently issued in paperback (Apex ed.; Nashville: Abingdon Press, 1951).

decidedly different backgrounds but motivated by gospel faith wrestled with the psychological insights offered in *Self-Understanding*, personages crumbled; persons began to emerge speaking the truth in love to one another. *Koinonia*, Christian fellowship, happened. We anticipate nothing less this year as we read Paul Tournier's *The Meaning of Persons*.[7]

"Books and Coffee" has been a splendid opportunity for persons to converse with persons, to communicate with one another rather than talk *at* each other. A widespread hunger for personal encounter and acceptance—a hunger which drives many lonely people into bars, illicit sex, and ruthless competition—is a complex part of our affluent, depersonalized culture. "Smooth" social gatherings and "rough" competitive living militate against meaningful personal encounters in the world; people are "on guard." Only God's Word through persons can create the social situation where lonely, anxious, aggressive personages, dropping their guard, actually feel free to be *persons*. And only God's Word through persons can shatter the insulation and penetrate the defenses of people who deliberately lose themselves in the round of business and social activities to escape knowing themselves and getting involved with other persons. Persons and personages come under the Word at "Books and Coffee"; the Holy Spirit moves among them, unmasking personages and creating a community of persons.

Another arena where Trinity's members wrestle with faith and life is provided by the Religious Drama Group. It is directed by a lay member whose avocation is the theater. The drama workshop attracts persons who wish to act, seeing in religious drama a vehicle for lay preaching and teaching in a secular

[7] (New York: Harper & Row, 1956). Since 1956 we have shared this remarkable book with seventy or so parishioners.

society. With this end in view, the director hopes to produce *The Sign of Jonah*. Twice this little band has brought the Theatre of Concern from New York to Trinity. Parishioners and others in the community have responded eagerly to *Old Ymir's Clay Pot, Joan and King Charlie,* and *What's the Big Idea?* On the other hand the periodic meetings of the drama group provide the opportunity to review and discuss contemporary plays and novels—*A Man for All Seasons, The Deputy, Summer and Smoke.* The lay leader, skilled in the theater and deeply involved in Christ's ministry through Trinity, guides the discussions toward creative encounters. These meetings increase the participants' awareness of the "lost" world, sharpen lay evangelism, and challenge nonmembers. Occasionally they provide a "moment of truth" for a casual member who, through the dialogues, perceives for the first time something of the gospel's relevance for the world.

The director of the drama group, the clergy, and laymen with special interests and skills also participate in a local venture, "Encounter," sponsored by the local theological seminary.[8] This venture has permanent meeting quarters in an informal coffee-house on a back street at the heart of the city. Concerned persons from the "church" and the "world" meet in dialogue on art, literature, race, housing, Roman-Protestant relationships, etc. It is a bit of leaven for the city. Trinity participates in and supports the venture appreciatively.

Another teaching experiment in the parish has proved to be meaningful to several hundred adults in Trinity—"Coffee and Conversation with the Clergy." Called for by the laity, the group met every second Sunday evening of each month during

[8] Lancaster Theological Seminary, United Church of Christ.

1963-64. Parishioners and their friends gathered in the parish house to converse with the clergy and with one another first on the sermons preached during the preceding four-week period and thereafter on any aspect of Christian faith and life.

The dynamic encounters at these meetings will be better appreciated in the context of Chapter 6, "Living Together at Trinity." These few sentences are simply descriptive. In the course of an evening—sixty to a hundred persons participating—forty to ninety exchanges occur between and among the parishioners themselves. The clergy act as catalytic agents, encouraging and guiding the spirited exchange of ideas and experiences. Most questions are allowed to remain "open end"; the margins of mystery around life, love, and faith are acknowledged. Critical minds are especially comfortable about speaking out in these gatherings, and certain prospective members are particularly invited. The dialogue on corporate guilt, initiated by a schoolteacher a week after President Kennedy's tragic death, translated the biblical doctrines of sin and grace into an existential encounter.

These are some of the special teaching situations which have been or are currently useful to the Holy Spirit in Trinity parish. Scores more exist in the women's circles, the weekly pastoral conversations with three to six persons—vestrymen, church school leaders, businessmen, professional people—oriented to the church's ministry in the world. The Friday noon services, reaching six hundred different persons, provide an impetus for these small, unannounced discussion groups where urban planning, family counseling, recreation, vocational training, open housing, and other questions are examined critically by concerned Christians. So the Word of the Lord is taught among Trinity's people in many ways at many hours other than the Sunday morning church school hour.

Another strand in Christian teaching in the parish has been the steady fostering of lay interest in theology as a tool for effective teaching and witnessing. The parish library was established primarily as a theological-biblical resource center. Among its titles are *The Interpreter's Bible*; *The Book of the Acts of God*, by G. Ernest Wright and Reginald H. Fuller; *Christian Faith Series*, Reinhold Niebuhr, consulting editor; *Luther: Early Theological Works*, edited by James Atkinson; *The Book of Concord*, edited by Theodore Tappert; Calvin's *Institutes of Christian Religion*, edited by John T. McNeill; *The Small Sects in America*, by Elmer T. Clark; *Christianity and Communism Today*, by John C. Bennett; *From the Stone Age to Christianity*, by William F. Albright; *The Theology of Dietrich Bonhoeffer*, by John D. Godsey; *The New Being*, by Paul Tillich; scholarly Christian biographies; works by Camus, Bruckberger, John Murray, and others. The books referred to throughout this report are available in the parish library or the libraries of the clergy. Several trained librarians (parishioners) administer the resource center at stated hours throughout the week. Expansive, well-appointed library and reading room facilities were created in the parish house during 1963. There, on all days of the week, committed Christians equip themselves to teach, preach, and evangelize more effectively. Some prefer to read and study during the church school hour; we consider this to be dialogue for them. An enthusiastic new member wrote:

Trinity continues to excite and surprise [my husband] and me. . . . I had occasion to go to the parish library. I couldn't believe it. . . .

There were works I hadn't seen since college days and many I hadn't read: Tillich, Bainton, Albright. . . . Good heavens! Do our members read those books? I borrowed Bainton on the spot.

Noncollege people use the parish library as frequently as college graduates, leaning heavily on *The Interpreter's Bible,* the Barclay studies, and concordances. Their favorite authors are Bainton, Harkness, Hiltner, Stewart, Thielicke, and Trueblood. We discovered that it is a mistake to assume that only college graduates will read substantial historical and theological studies. One layman, a high school graduate, reads extensively in the field of history—*The Image of America,* Eric Goldman's *Rendezvous with Destiny,* Churchill's memoirs, and George F. Kennan on American foreign policy! A middle-aged counselee read profitably J. S. Whale's *Victor and Victim.* John Baillie's *Diary of Private Prayer* is in eighty parish homes. Reinhold Niebuhr's *Faith and History* and Paul Tournier's *The Meaning of Persons* have provided enlightenment for sixty or so noncollege counselees as well as for a hundred college-trained persons. Helmut Thielicke's *The Ethics of Sex,* published in 1964, is currently finding its way into parish homes. Not everyone will read Bruckberger, Camus, Niebuhr, Thielicke, Tournier, and Whale. But every parishioner should get the opportunity to discover for himself what he can and will read.

The notion, widely held in church circles, that laymen will not read serious books is contrary to our experience in Trinity. The parish library and the local theological seminary library are used. One parishioner, a professor of biology at Franklin and Marshall College, is convinced that he has borrowed "more books from the seminary library than any biologist in history!" Another parishioner, asked to present the life of Francis of

Assisi in the circles of the Lutheran Church Women, researched in twenty-three general and special works to prepare her splendid lecture. Serious authors and modern translators have gained many friends at Trinity: Gordon W. Allport, Baillie, John C. Bennett, Bonhoeffer, Bruckberger, Brunner, Camus, Goodspeed, Herberg, Hiltner, Daniel Jenkins, Jung, Kierkegaard, Marty, Ronald Knox, Moffatt, Andrew Murray, Richard and Reinhold Niebuhr, Phillips, David E. Roberts, Sartre, Schlesinger, Tillich, Tournier, R. F. Weymouth, Whale, and Daniel D. Williams.

The ministry of good reading is not a one-way street. Laymen have introduced their clergy to exciting books in many fields, among them Bruckberger's *The Image of America,* Highet's *The Art of Teaching,* David Head's *Stammerer's Tongue,* and Walter Kaufmann's *The Faith of a Heretic.* It is not unusual for Trinity's members to thank one another for the introduction to Tournier's *Guilt and Grace,* Camus' *The Fall,* or Steinbeck's *Travels with Charley.* The clergy are the grateful recipients of many good books with the little note, "Thank you for.... Thought you'd appreciate a copy of...."

The parish is also encouraged to attend the open lectures offered at several local colleges and the theological seminary. Some do attend and are enriched, and discuss their new insights with others. A corporation executive was persuaded to attend a local lecture by Paul Tillich; he returned asking for books by that eminent theologian. A research engineer relies heavily on Tillich's works in witnessing among his intellectual colleagues in and beyond Lancaster. A medical doctor has been captivated by Tournier. A wife and mother credits Camus with making her an evangelist. Presently, Rolf Hochhuth's *The Deputy,* preached on twice in 1964, has stirred lively discussions in the parish.

The impasse between theology and activism in Trinity is dented, if not broken. Theology has not replaced contract bridge, nor has the theological discussion group supplanted the cocktail hour; but doctrine and dialogue are in style in many quarters of the parish. A regiment of trained, equipped soldiers are doing battle for the Lord. Trinity Church can sing "Onward Christian Soldiers" with some integrity as well as gusto.

————CHAPTER 5————

DYNAMICS FOR OUTREACH

I should like to see some results among you.

—ROMANS 1:11 (PHILLIPS)

First a few recruits and then many Christian soldiers—persuaded by gospel preaching to enlist in Christ's army and learning the ways of effective spiritual warfare through evangelical
teaching—examined evangelism, stewardship, and the sacraments in their relationship to Christian worship and Christian
education. The essence of those innumerable dialogues and encounters oriented to three fundamental questions. Is Christian
evangelism a human activity, or is it the born-again congregation's proper witness to Christ? Is Christian stewardship a human program for raising the local budget, or the congregation's
responsible custodianship of the gospel? Are the sacraments

proofs of church membership, cultic rites, or channels of God's renewing power? How the soldiers arrived at their answers from the manual, on the drill field, and in combat is the theme of this chapter.

Evangelism

The parish discovered in worship, study, and firsthand experience that the evangelist's dynamic stems from his personal relationship with Christ. The parishioners discovered also that the Christian evangelist must understand his culture or see his witness blunted. First, the love of Christ persuaded some to evangelize. Then they learned in hard experience that simply telling the "old, old story of Jesus and his love" is not enough to win a hearing for the gospel. Disheartening personal failures and a congregation-wide fiasco in evangelistic work convinced the clergy and lay leaders that unless the Word possesses the evangelist, there is no witness to Christ; and equally, unless the evangelist understands his cultural situation, his witness will be blunted or aborted.

Today's Christian has not only the task of commending the gospel to those whom Friedrich Schleiermacher called its "cultured despisers" and to those whom Kierkegaard said "had done away with Christianity without being aware of it," but also to the many displaced persons who have no knowledge of the Christian God at all. The disposition in some evangelical circles to exhort clergy and laity to simply "preach the gospel" has hurt rather than helped the church's potential witness. Paul preached Christ crucified, but he borrowed shamelessly from Judaism and Hellenism to proclaim this glad, good news. Paul understood both cultures. Luther understood some—certainly not all—of the cultural realities of sixteenth-century Europe.

Wesley had a vivid picture of displaced persons in the changing society of eighteenth-century Britain. Dietrich Bonhoeffer was a cultural realist as well as a believer. Christian witnessing has always required faith in, knowledge of, and obedience to God and his ways in his world.

Since the difficulties encountered in witnessing to this generation root deep in the crisis of our culture, we decided that the parishioners should be challenged to recognize not only the crisis but its antecedents.[1] Essentially this is what many discussed, discerned, and some faced up to.

The sweeping social critiques of Nietzsche and Marx in the nineteenth century had fallen in the fertile soil of a deteriorating historical situation in the West. Two devastating world wars, an enervating economic depression that shook the social foundations of the industrial nations, the terrible rise of totalitarian states, the advent of nuclear weapons, Asia in ferment, and Africa in violent revolt—all this, we observed, had disheartened and in some quarters had overwhelmed the institutional church. These towering defeats, linked with the secularization of life inside the church in the West, made it appear that Carlyle's sweeping judgment—Christ has had his day—had been fulfilled, and that Nietzsche's call for the revision of values was a valid one. The parish leaders concluded that one cannot witness effectively if he is unaware of these awesome cultural problems or disdains theology.

On the other hand, we sought to keep our perspective. We recalled how the church had moved into every corner of the world during the nineteenth century; that the ecumenical movement, significant biblical studies, a theological renaissance, and a rising tide of healthy self-criticism were "signs of hope"

[1] See Chapter 3, note 1.

in the twentieth-century church; and that the American parish is a reality, its equipment and personnel immediately at hand.[2]

Slowly, unevenly, the members began to appreciate that they were called to live in the land of the Philistines—loving them, understanding them, speaking their language but declining to worship their gods (success, money, sex, pleasure, war) and witnessing in word and deed to the God who comes "eyeball to eyeball" in Jesus Christ. We were also learning that the church must listen as well as proclaim, dialogue as well as indoctrinate. Today Trinity listens to Camus and Sartre, Tennessee Williams and Arthur Miller, John O'Hara and Allen Drury, Walter Kaufmann and Harry Overstreet, Freud and Jung, Nietzsche and Marx, learning from them how to present the Christ in whom resides the true meaning and purpose of life. It is exceedingly difficult to witness effectively to postmodern man. The lay evangelist must be trained for battle as well as persuaded of the power of his weaponry—the Word.[3]

As the spirit of God brooded over the congregation and infiltrated human hearts during those first years, certain parishioners who appeared to be sensitive to God's claims and increasingly alert to cultural realities received this invitation to go out two-by-two as Christ's ambassadors.

You are among the eighty couples in Trinity's large membership receiving this invitation. . . . This is not another organization. It has no

---

[2] Elton Trueblood's *Signs of Hope in a Century of Despair* (New York: Harper & Row, 1950) was shared with some parishioners in those days. A year or so later, Kenneth Scott Latourette's *The Christian World Mission in Our Day* (New York: Harper & Brothers, 1954) provided the clergy with a concise statement for teaching purposes.

[3] Throughout these twelve years Trinity's clergy and a few laymen have used profitably H. Richard Niebuhr's *Christ and Culture* (New York: Harper & Brothers, 1951; Torchbooks ed.; Harper & Row, 1956), especially Chapters 1, 5, and 6.

officers. It is an affair of the spirit with a single purpose: winning persons to Christ through his church to help him exercise his ministry through his church.

The Seventy will accept these rules of spiritual obedience: (1) daily prayer for the worldwide church as well as for Trinity; (2) daily prayer for our lapsed members and the unchurched in our city; (3) faithful participation in the worship services; (4) visits in ten or twelve homes during each year—the names of these persons to be visited will come from the office and carry observations, suggestions, etc.; (5) visits to any number of homes *you* determine; (6) deliberate effort to *find* the unchurched and bring them as your guests to Trinity Church—any Sunday *you* choose; (7) alertness to special needs among our members and prompt notification of the pastor; (8) a steady appraisal of our emerging congregational program and constructive comments on its strengths and limitations. May our gracious Lord gain your whole-hearted acceptance.

No pressure was brought to bear on anyone. There was no cajoling, coaxing, or bargaining. Seventy-seven couples accepted the invitation and were commissioned. They worked for a season without meetings, group training sessions, or organized thrusts into the community. Individual teaching sessions were conducted by appointment in the homes or at the church office. Periodically, the Seventy received pastoral letters, teaching biblical evangelism and encouraging them in their spiritual disciplines. Occasionally, the pastoral letters included the names of several members who (1) communed regularly but worshiped sporadically; (2) communed rarely; (3) had not been near the church in years; (4) were new in the church. Only when the evangelists appeared to be ready to present the claims of Christ in the world were the names of prospectives included in the pastoral letters. The Seventy were also asked to attend a series of new members' classes. All cooperated, some attending four different series.

After a year of individual instruction and firsthand experience with lay visitation in the parish the Seventy were invited to participate in group training sessions. There the theology of evangelism and the cultural situation were reviewed; differences in the levels of the evangelists' faith, biblical knowledge, theological orientation, cultural awareness, and personal persuasiveness were recognized openly, admitted to, and discussed; the common objections advanced by unchurched persons were examined and discussed; mimeographed material describing ways into membership—adult baptism, confirmation, letter, reaffirmation—were provided; specific satisfactions and frustrations experienced by the lay evangelists were shared and scrutinized; to each of the seventy-seven couples was presented a copy of George Sweazey's *Effective Evangelism.*[4] Throughout their three years' service the Seventy were allowed to work at their own pace. They were encouraged to discover for themselves how the Holy Spirit uses disciplined human efforts to win persons to Christ through his church for the exercise of his ministry. They were undergirded by the church as they also discovered that Christian witnessing is not measured by results—often meager in our culture—but by the evangelist's fidelity to the Word.

During the Seventy's three years' service their visits in and beyond the parish (a) awakened many and matured some; wearied others and alienated a few; (b) strengthened the communing membership from one thousand to twelve hundred; (c) enlarged the average attendance at the worship services by several hundred persons; (d) stemmed the tide among younger

[4] (New York: Harper & Row, 1953). Very useful.

families who were disposed to transfer; (e) brought forward a substantial corps of new members; and (f) contributed to the emergence of Trinity's new image in the community. The results were not spectacular, but they were solid.

After four years' experience with the Word in preaching and teaching and the sacraments, and three years' experience with the Seventy, the parish leaders judged that the congregation was ready for "organization evangelism." A vestry committee set up the district plan of evangelism—seventeen districts covering an area of thirty-six square miles, with a deacon and several assistants presiding over each district. Our hopes were high. But the venture proved to be ill-advised. The number of parishioners assigned, eighty-five to one hundred, was unmanageable for those greathearted lay evangelists. They were frustrated by mechanics and masses; they preferred the style and pace of the Seventy. In spite of our efforts to scrutinize methods we were engaged in a programmatic venture. A mistake in judgment was admitted by the ordained and lay leaders, and a fresh approach promised.

Simple adaptation of the tempting district plan or a return to the more tempting Seventy were no longer the meaningful courses at Trinity. The mind and spirit of the congregation was being transformed by the Holy Spirit. Evangelism was becoming spontaneous as well as disciplined. Members, maturing in the faith, were (a) worshiping expectantly every Sunday; (b) inviting guests and finding prospective members; (c) discussing sermons at home, work, and social gatherings; and (d) beginning to practice the Christian stewardship of money. This changing mind in the parish would eventually push benevolence far beyond "quotas" and bring a hundred and fifty new people

into Trinity annually. These typical responses from three parishioners illustrate this changing congregational mind.

Ours is not an optional God, an elective. . . . Navy experience taught
us vividly that church attendance is no meager witness. It was the
subject of many conversations. . . . my husband was the only Protestant
officer on his destroyer to attend church regularly. We were amused
when people felt obliged to explain to us why they didn't manage a
better record for themselves. . . . Church attendance is witness. . . . It
is an active form of evangelism.

So often I have left a service in Trinity stirred to the depths of my
soul with a great desire to thank you for the truth you have brought to
my heart. While I have thanked God, I have failed to thank his servant.
Without any "gushing" I will say that the message today coupled with
Bach's B Minor Mass was a wonderful event in my life. It left me only
with the regret that I didn't *bring anyone with me*.

The Seventy are making dignified Trinity into a fanatics club. . . .
The vestry has lost its mind to allow such things to be fostered in
historic Trinity. Next, we'll be greeting each other with, "Brother, are
you saved?"

Seeking to channel this new spirit in Trinity, we decided that
inreach should be emphasized once again. The undershepherding
program was outlined, authorized, launched. Seventy-three districts with fifteen homes each were defined geographically by
an experienced lay evangelist from the Seventy, who also chaired
the undershepherding teams of husband and wife. The districts
were geographically small, and wherever possible the undershepherd served in his own neighborhood. Twenty of the twenty-
one vestrymen became undershepherds. The lay chairman,
clergy, and guest lecturers, such as Elton Trueblood, led the

semiannual meetings at which practical concerns in shepherding were studied and discussed. Eighty-nine of the one hundred forty undershepherds chose to be Yokefellows.[5]

One year the undershepherds, having received mimeographed source materials from the clergy, conducted Bible study groups in their homes. Parish response was uneven, but results could be discerned. Six hundred persons participated; some new families were won to the practice of daily Bible study; practitioners, encouraged to keep at it, improved their skills; several Bible study groups came into being spontaneously.

The undershepherds also accepted responsibility in their districts for advising the clergy of hospitalization, illness in a home, need for the homemaker's service, nonattendance at worship, unbaptized children, children not in the church school, teenagers not attending the Luther League and/or catechetical classes, real economic need, theological concern, and severe dissatisfaction concerning some area of church life. They were also responsible for providing opportunities for Christian fellowship among the members in their districts, engaging in visitation in their little "parish," shepherding the careless, and seeking out and reporting prospective members. In the projects in which the clergy were not advised the undershepherds were guided through the following memo from the church office.

Memo to Undershepherds, District _____ Date _____
    ( ) New members _____
    ( ) Home from hospital _____
    ( ) Death in the family _____
    ( ) Recently married _____

[5] The Yokefellows agree to daily prayer, daily Scripture study, regular worship, planned giving, daily witness, and theological study.

( ) New baby in the family _____
( ) Has not communed this year_____
( ) Irregular church attendance _____
( ) Prospective members _____
( ) Other information _____

Looking back, we conclude that the undershepherds' most significant service was in person-to-person interviews, intimate shepherding in their parishes, group discussions, Bible study, and occasional social affairs, such as picnics, coffees, and desserts. The spirit and character of their ministry are revealed through these several lay reports, written by undershepherds themselves.

Case 1

Mrs. A.: I have often thought I'd like to go over to the [suburban church] some Sunday.

Undershepherd: Do you find it hard to get into Trinity?

Mrs. A.: Oh, no, I drive, but Trinity is so big, and I think the people are so cold. You see—I don't make friends easily. (She then began a long speech about the people who sit in "their" pew even though the rental system is no longer in existence. She said some people will practically sit on your lap, if they must, in order to get the same seat each Sunday.)

Undershepherd: Well, have you ever gone to any of the circle meetings?

Mrs. A.: I did join, but I haven't been able to attend any of the meetings; something always comes up. Mrs. _____ keeps calling me every month.

Undershepherd: Perhaps if you could get out to some of those and get to meet some of the women, you would feel more at home. Your neighbor across the street is in my circle. If you'd like to come along, we'd be happy to stop by and pick you up. (Time, programs, transportation, and other plans for circle meetings were then discussed.)

Mrs. A.: No, thank you, I did join another circle; and I think if I go to any, I'd better go to that one.

Undershepherd: Do give it a try, and I hope you'll come to the coffee hour on March 12. This would be a good chance to get acquainted with some of the other members.

Mrs. A.: I'll try to make it.

P. S. *She did not attend.*

Case 2

Mr. A.: How did you react to the open forum at Trinity on the Kennedy religious matter?

Undershepherd: I found it instructive and am grateful to be in a church that speaks on confused issues in society. Did you know that the vestry issued a statement in support of it?

Mr. A.: Yes, and I'm glad to be in Trinity too. I travel widely, and everywhere I find so much religious bigotry . . . vicious.

Undershepherd: You joined Trinity recently, I understand from the church office.

Mr. A.: Yes, I was a _____ before joining here. You know, I'll never get used to that formal service at eleven o'clock in spite of the lecture on it in the New Members' Class.

Undershepherd: I've attended those classes. Everyone doesn't have to worship the same way, and Trinity offers four different kinds of services. The important thing is to receive the Word of God. . . . Why did you change denominations and join Trinity?

Mr. A.: We've moved three times because of my work. I went to Sunday school as a youth but never joined a church until I married. When I moved to another city, we joined a community church. In the next city we were _____. We have chosen each church for its preaching. But here for the first time we are finding that all parts of the church are strong. Our kids are learning so much. We've borrowed books from the parish library, and we're learning all the time. I hope I don't have to move.

Trinity's undershepherds were good ministers of Jesus Christ. They gladdened his gallant heart, shepherding persons in his behalf. They served from 1957 until 1963, and their creative participation in Trinity's renewal was incalculable. But every organized work of the Spirit is reviewed periodically in parishes alert to exercising Christ's ministry. Trinity had not made any organized evangelistic thrust into the community during the twentieth century, except for the abortive effort, 1956-57. After a decade of working on inreach and letting outreach be spontaneous, we judged that the parish was ready for disciplined outreach. We had the resources: several hundred seasoned evangelists; five hundred parishioners who witnessed sporadically; a parish accustomed to venturing; lay members in every corner of metropolitan Lancaster and in every stratum of society; and a lay assistant—responsible for census, survey, assignments, and coordination—who had special knowledge of and experience with the necessary mechanics for organized outreach.

The new thrust is under way. The first area surveyed—Trinity's "front yard"—showed 30 percent unchurched persons. A second survey in another downtown area, accomplished in cooperation with several other downtown churches, pointed up another field for evangelism. Continuing census and survey, singly or in cooperation with other congregations, are planned for other parts of metropolitan Lancaster over a three-year period. A foray into the first field surveyed called thirty-one participants into the new members' class, twenty-three of whom united with the congregation. Sixteen of these new members had no prior church affiliation. During 1963, Trinity's lay evangelists made hundreds of person-to-person contacts, and their disciplined witness brought one hundred and ninety persons into Christ's church that year.

The current venture in evangelistic work is designed to place and use experienced evangelists in every corner of metropolitan Lancaster. It also aims to have the experienced evangelists teach other willing persons in their districts how to evangelize. Unlike the Seventy and the undershepherds, this group—the Order of St. Andrew—is geared primarily to outreach. They meet periodically for Bible study, discussion of their work, and training sessions. The lay chairman of the former undershepherds—a business executive who began in 1954 with the Seventy—continues to serve, defining districts, assigning couples, receiving reports. The staff lay assistant directs the ongoing census and survey and works closely with the evangelists. Another vestry committee and two staff members welcome and shepherd those who unite with Trinity's congregation. An ordained staff member is responsible for the pastoral care of the evangelists. The Order of St. Andrew at Trinity serves Christ not chiefly because it is well-ordered but because its personnel are converted to Christ, equipped to be his ambassadors, and cared for pastorally. This required a decade, and the task is not finished; pastoral care is required constantly. Some evangelists get "weary in well-doing." There are "John Marks" who quit, later to try again; and occasionally there is a "Demas" who simply quits cold.

If prospective members are shepherded into the born-again parish by a rising corps of lay evangelists, these candidates for the kingdom must be acquainted with what Christ expects of them in his church. The new members' class was a splendid legacy at Trinity. This established teaching opportunity was seized eagerly. The time was changed to Sunday mornings during the church school hour. The name was changed to the Inquirers' Class, with each prospective being advised that he was not expected to "join" simply because he came to class. Trinity's members, rooted shallowly in biblical and confessional faith, were urged repeatedly to attend a series of classes. More than half the original thousand communicants did attend; and since prospective members are required to attend the classes, 80 percent of Trinity's present communing membership have been exposed to a study of Christian liturgy, history, and doctrine during these lectures.

From 1952 until 1963, two series of classes in the spring and autumn were conducted annually, meeting on five consecutive Sunday mornings during the church school hour. Questions from the floor were handled during the sessions. The lectures were on this order.

Lecture I

WHY WE WORSHIP AS WE DO. An hour's study of the liturgy—its biblical character and historical antecedents—together with a brief description of Matins, Vespers, the Friday noonday services, the Suffrages. The liturgy viewed as a vehicle for worship. Discussion of the sermon and offering as acts of worship.

Lecture II

HOW THE CHURCH AND BIBLE CAME TO BE. A brief historical appraisal and discussion of (a) the church antedating the Scriptures; (b) canonical Scriptures, manuscripts, translations, manual productions; (c) the meaning of the Scriptures as witness to the Word; (d) myth, legend, story, prophets, the historical Jesus, the Resurrection Christ.

Lecture III

THE MEDIEVAL CHURCH AND THE PROTESTANT REFORMATION. A historical appraisal of both "churches" with emphasis on (a) the catholicity of the church and its apostolic character; (b) the precursors of the Reformation; (c) Luther's conversion experience and growth in grace; his step-by-step experience in the faith from 1517 (theses) through Worms (1521), marriage (1525), and the *Augsburg Confession* (1530); (d) the basic difference between Romanism and Protestantism: "Where does authority reside?" (e) the *Augsburg Confession;* (f) the Lutheran Church—apostolic, catholic, confessional.

Lecture IV

LUTHER'S SMALL CATECHISM. Why it was written; the creeds of Christendom; discussion of the Apostles' Creed, the Lord's Prayer, infant baptism, the Lord's Supper (transubstantiation, memorial, "real presence"), and the Ten Commandments (interpreted and applied to life situations in the light of the gospel); the meaning of "evangelical."

Lecture V

LIFE IN TRINITY PARISH. History, worship, Christian education, evangelism, stewardship, the missionary thrust, social action, staff ministry, *koinonia,* and the "margins of mystery."

The series of classes was increased from two to four annually in 1963 because Trinity's members and staff were calling up a steady stream of candidates. Presently, the new members are encouraged to attend "Coffee and Conversation with the Clergy" for a year so that they can air their questions, express their differences, and be exposed to Trinity's style of dialogue and indoctrination. Each new member receives a four-page statement of the twenty-eight articles of the *Augsburg Confession,* a copy of Luther's *Small Catechism,* and an interpretative historical booklet on Trinity. New members are advised concerning translations of the Scriptures and several works on church history.[6]

[6] Walter Russell Bowie, *The Story of the Church* (Nashville: Abingdon Press, 1955) and Charles M. Jacobs, *The Story of the Church* (Philadelphia: Fortress Press, 1925) are suggested. Translations—the Revised Standard Version and Phillips— are runaway favorites. We encourage some parishioners to use Ronald Knox's translation of the New Testament.

Our experience convinces us that the parish must instruct its candidates for membership. We are equally convinced that the new members' class, enthusiastically endorsed by many churches today, offers no magic formula for parish renewal. Unless the teaching in the classes is essential and existential, the worship services relevant, teaching-learning-serving opportunities offered, and the new members shepherded according to their needs, the class becomes another parish activity insulating persons against the reality of God.

Gospel preaching, evangelical teaching, and lay evangelism persuaded eighteen hundred persons from all walks of life to stand before the altar in Trinity and declare themselves for Christ. Like the Rainbow Division of World War I these recruits represent the different strata of society. They are: uneducated, uncultured, emotionally motivated people who sense that Christ is their best hope—the face of Trinity parish is no longer bland nor all-white; counselees, a third of the new members, from all walks of life who desire fellowship with the Christ who cared for them in their time of sore distress; intellectuals who never belonged to the church or, having been members in their youth, drifted or turned away; young people, fifteen to thirty years of age, who are attracted to a congregation which faces the problems inherent in dating, courtship, marriage, childbearing, and family living; many new residents in Lancaster from all denominations; a handful of persons from local churches whose motives for transfer appear to be wholesome; a few who turn out to be like Red Skelton's "Freddie the Freeloader," convinced that they can belong for nothing and do little because, as they put it, "the wagon is rolling." Because Trinity's laity are constrained to witness and have learned to do it effectively, the communing membership, in spite of deaths and heavy transfers through a mobile membership in an industrial community, has grown steadily from 1,018 to 1,700. Attendance at worship has climbed from an average 300 to an average 1,350, including the Friday noon service; and the church's witness is heard in all corners of community life.

There are, of course, prospectives in the classes who do not unite with Trinity congregation. They recoil from the demands of Christ. Like the rich young ruler, some go away sorrowing. Like Nicodemus, some go away intellectually offended. Like the Pharisees, a few go away spreading falsehoods. This minority, exercising their freedom, continue to bypass the church or unite casually with a congregation which makes fewer demands on them as persons.

There are also people who do not have the temperament to mature in Christ in a large downtown church. They are more likely to mature in the faith in a smaller neighborhood parish. Alerted to this temperament, Trinity's lay evangelists are instructed to encourage such persons to seek membership in a congregation other than Trinity. It is unrealistic to suggest that one church is as good as another for everyone. As persons differ sharply in temperament and in their capacity for involvement, even so do congregations differ in their effective witness to God's Word and in their style of witness. These differences should be recognized, respected, and honored by the clergy *and* lay evangelists. The church exists not to get members, but to win persons to Christ. In this practical orientation to the church as mission the ecumenical spirit is truly exhibited.

Some people decline to unite with Trinity's congregation at the close of a series of classes because they are not ready to commit themselves unreservedly. Most of these continue to worship; some make counseling appointments; perhaps half unite eventually with the church. Among the hundred or so who came into Trinity hesitantly, critically—attending several series of classes—were a one-time Mennonite tradesman who had not attended church in years, a Roman Catholic professional man, a skyrocketing business executive. These men—and others like them, who counted the cost of discipleship before declaring, "Lord, Lord"—have been powerful leaven in the congregation's new life.

Tensions are induced by Trinity's procedures on membership. Some people, discouraged from joining, decline to tell or are emotionally unable to relate the truth about the classes or the personal interviews. And here and there an unconverted congregation pretends to despise what it declines to emulate. But would any student of the New Testament and contemporary culture expect it to be otherwise? The born-again congregation, seeking to orient to God's purposes, collides inevitably with any person or institution orienting to a human purpose. Only in those congregations which accept God's authority can the Holy Spirit, who works through the Word, persuade sin-sick people to respond to Christ's appeal and thereafter allow Christ, in righteous love, to appeal through their persons to other persons. Christian congregations do not covet plaudits from a religionized culture; they yearn and labor to transform that culture by converting those who fashion and sustain it.

If teaching evangelism in Trinity parish and equipping persons to witness in the world were often tedious and frustrating, teaching stewardship was exciting but exhausting.

Stewardship

Lancaster—steeped in Pennsylvania Dutch culture—is stable, often to the point of rigidity. And "Old Trinity" was at home in Lancaster. The two appeared to be inextricably bound together. The parish leaders, looking back on 1952-57, shake their heads and say, "Trinity was a hard nut to crack." It was indeed. Our experience inclines us to the view that the New England Yankee must yield to the Pennsylvania Dutchman on keeping both his traditions and his money!

Trinity's material way of looking at life was rooted in generations of frugal living. The official records reveal that the vestry refused in 1801 to contribute any money for the establishment of a Lutheran theological school in the United States; Trinity had to pay for its new tower and steeple. Finally the congregation got the state legislature to sanction a lottery which helped to clear the debt.[7] Theological education went begging; steeples, farms, and businesses came first. This same attitude, hard as steel, characterized the congregation at mid-twentieth century. Current expenditures were kept to an unrealistic minimum; the modest apportionment had not been paid in full for several years. One thousand communicants were giving little more than $30,000 a year for the total *current* work of a downtown church. A disproportionate share of that sum was used to maintain a large church building, a dilapidated parish house, a separate boiler house, and a parsonage.

The new pastor entered into the hardships of his predecessors who had also addressed themselves to this ingrained temper of mind. Their accomplishments were significant: money-making schemes had been outlawed, the practice of pledging was in force, and precise records were maintained. But the congregation was not exercising its proper stewardship of the gospel. During those first difficult years, therefore, we emphasized that stewardship is *not* a device for raising a current budget or pay-

[7] An original lottery ticket is on display in Trinity's historical museum.

ing benevolence in full; it is not a parish activity to be promoted by a stewardship committee. Calling the congregation before the tribunal of biblical evidence, we emphasized that stewardship is every Christian's custodianship of the glorious gospel of God; all baptized persons are stewards, and the issue is whether God considers them responsible or irresponsible in the exercise of that stewardship. The interminable dialogues, heated debates, and painful confrontations called forth these biblical insights.

Jesus did not ask his followers to withdraw from the world; he encouraged them to accept gladly God's creation and use it joyously to reveal his love. The Incarnation demonstrated the validity of this fundamental truth in the book of Genesis: God loves what he creates, wayward though it be, and knows its genuine worth in Christ. Jesus, enabling man to recover his true humanity, teaches him how to distinguish between persons and things without despising either. The fundamental fault in the foolish farmer was that he supposed he could secure his person through material holdings. The fault in the rich young ruler was not in his having great wealth but in his disposition to value his person in terms of it. Whoever accepts Christ as the Lord of all life is enabled to handle things in the interest of persons and to realize his true humanity without using persons as means. This was one strand in teaching stewardship.

Another strand had to do with discipline, a distasteful word in a culture which equates liberty with license. Admitting that an occasional convert like Zacchaeus experiences God's forgiveness so overwhelmingly that his renewed life cascades redemptively into society, we recognized that most people mature in the faith through disciplined responses to God: regular worship, daily study, deliberate witness, planned giving. Today, the members in Trinity who give beyond their means, and some do, come from the ranks of those disciplined givers.

We also declined to emphasize benevolence giving as a shot in the arm for current giving. That approach struck us as being wickedly calculating. The Word does not foster an "ours" and "theirs" mentality; it drives to the heart of the contemporary church's problem: provincialism and selfishness. These twin evils must be tackled on cultural and spiritual grounds; the Christian stewardship of time, talent, and goods rest on the *enlightened mind* and the *converted heart*. Programs and campaigns, carefully planned and skillfully executed, can add dollars to church budgets, but only the Holy Spirit can convert persons to be Christian stewards.

So the Word of the Lord began to renew Trinity. Current expenditures climbed steadily from $30,000 to $125,000 annually. Parish benevolence increased ninefold—$14,000 to $100,000 annually. The budget has been *overmatched* each year since 1957. Except for placing a new organ in 1962, there have been no special appeals in the parish since 1953. The overage from current giving has provided the means to complete and fully furnish the parish house, increase staff personnel, add a new boiler unit, purchase two additional downtown properties for future expansion, and enlarge the parking facilities. Because Christ is being received hospitably in hundreds of hearts, Trinity parish is learning to exercise an imaginative custodianship of the gospel and, in the process, is involving its talents, time, energy, and money. This is Christian stewardship.

But person-to-person teaching in this no man's land requires emotional resilience, common sense, and courage in the clergy and lay leaders. The clergy cannot do the task alone. On the other hand, they have no right to delegate it to the laity alone or ask outsiders to do it for them. It is a pastoral responsibility. Breaking the culture barrier, obliterating the color line, and breaching the wall between worship and social action evoked less hostility in Trinity than teaching Christian stewardship among the members. Meeting a benevolence quota and expanding a current budget can be managed by religious organization men; only converted persons will confront other persons in church and society about money for Christ's sake.

Because money is an extension of one's person, and the earning and spending of it binds one to or alienates him from Christ, teaching the Christian stewardship of it calls for intimate, sometimes tense, personal encounters. At best, conflict is inevitable. An irate parishioner phoned after an encounter with a fellow member at a cocktail party. This was his complaint:

We were discussing foreign aid. I said Democrats have no money sense. _____ disagreed strongly. . . . One word led to another. . . . Suddenly he got into what he calls Christian giving and said the problems in the world are rooted in human selfishness. . . . He challenged my frequent absences from church—said the church would disappear if everybody acted as I do. . . . Somewhere I said that I did not agree with preaching stewardship. He said I didn't understand the gospel of Jesus Christ. . . . Really, it was quite embarrassing.

The disciples were becoming witnesses. The domesticated gospel was breaking out of Trinity into the cocktail hour! A religionized culture was discovering that the gospel brings both fire and sword.

God's Word, confronting persons in their freedom, disturbs and alienates some; it persuades others. One layman, a tither from his youth, felt constrained to talk about giving with a fellow member who was also his client—a rather delicate meeting some of us thought. Nevertheless, the conversation took place with these unexpected results: the client's family now worships regularly instead of sporadically; the weekly gift was increased substantially; the professional relationship was not disrupted. The gallant heart of Jesus Christ was gladdened by that man's bold witness; the clergy and other parish leaders hastened to reexamine their own hesitant approaches. The following undershepherd's report shows how some laymen in Trinity go about teaching stewardship.

Mr. A.: Does Trinity's budget really come from average income people like us?

Undershepherd: It does. Salaried people provide 98 percent of the budget. I'm a vestryman, as you know, and I can tell you that the highest gift is $50 weekly and comes from a man whose family is dependent on his earnings. Another member I know is a clerk in a store who gives $5 weekly. Both are tithers. We have a hundred or so, I think.

Mr. A.: Do you believe in tithing?

Undershepherd: I believe in it and do it on my income.

Mr. A.: But why? We have a hard time on my income. Why should we tithe? You're telling me I should.

Undershepherd: Friend, you brought up the subject, but I do feel strongly about it. You imply that the church has no right to talk to us about money. We should give freely because we receive everything from God. The church must say that.

Mr. A.: I can't afford to give much.

Undershepherd: No one in Trinity ever tells anyone how much to give.

Mr. A.: Yes they do. They want you to tithe. That's saying that if we don't, we aren't doing our part.

Undershepherd: That isn't true. "It's Christ who matters in stewardship. The tithe is the first reasonable step in Christian giving." I've heard that a hundred times in Trinity; I believe it.

Mr. A.: But tithing is legalistic—it's from the Old Testament.

Undershepherd: No, it is disciplined response to God's goodness.

Mr. A.: Do all vestrymen give a lot? Do the ministers tithe?

Undershepherd: Each year the Stewardship Committee gives us a list of vestry and staff gifts—without names. The weekly gifts range from $4 a Sunday to $50 a Sunday. Every vestryman is on earned income; the ministers tithe. We think we should do what we ask others to do. Christianity gives me a different view of life. That's why I'm talking with you.

Mr. A.: I've been thinking about that. Why does he bother with me? And you come right to the point. I like that. We'll think about it.

Undershepherd: Good, it is important. You should think and talk and pray about it.

Memo: I wrote this because it is one of the best visits I ever made. ———— later phoned to say he and his wife talked about our visit and finally decided to increase their giving substantially. I've gotten some new members for Trinity, but somehow this visit and its outcome are most rewarding. Perhaps because I once thought as he thought.

Pastors and people should be encouraged to handle the task of teaching stewardship themselves. Trinity's parish leaders declined to rely on outsiders for help or to look for readily supplied programs. Orienting to the biblical image of the ministry, we decided that there is no substitute for the Word's confrontation of persons through persons in teaching Christian stewardship and that these confrontations should not be delegated to others. We decided that it was necessary for Trinity to break its bondage to a naturalistic culture which views the solution of all problems in terms of manipulating not only technical powers but persons. We agreed that Trinity parish, if it were to break that bondage, had to recover God's purpose for his church —the transformation of persons through the Word in preaching, teaching, and the sacraments. Forgetting results, we inquired urgently, therefore, about conversion, new life, and social responsibility in the parish. This was our strategy in teaching stewardship.

If the church wants to be in dialogue with the world, it must first admit and face up to its own desperate need for conversion, repent, and let God's Word bring healing where it will. Because Trinity's annual budget has climbed steadily from $43,000 to $225,000, the church office receives numerous requests for literature, programs, techniques. We have none. The key to Trinity's practice of stewardship is not in the economic results but in the parish's deliberate rejection of programmatic stewardship in favor of a patient reliance on God's Word in preaching and teaching and personal confrontation. The Holy Spirit motivates persons to be responsible stewards. Stewardship is a fruit of parish renewal.

The Sacraments

The impasse between theology and activism in Trinity parish was strikingly evident in the parishioners' attitudes toward the sacraments. And what church members actually believe about the sacraments is a key to their understanding of the Word of God. If that delightful little book, *O Ye Jigs & Juleps,* had been published in 1952 instead of 1963, this bit from its opening page would have introduced one of the several early sermons on the sacraments.

Sacraments are what you do in Church. What you do at home is something else. . . .

When you are little and ugly somebody carries you in church on a pillow, and you come out a child of God and inheritor of the Kingdom of Heaven. They pour water on your head and that's a sacrament. . . .

Only I left out the bread and wine. That's a sacrament too. I tasted some of that bread in the choir room and it tasted just like my gold fish wafers.[8]

Our teaching on the sacraments, carried on in the context of worship and oriented to the Word, began with church history. The medieval church, it was pointed out, exalted the sacraments at the expense of gospel preaching and teaching. The mainstream of the Reformation, except for some enthusiasts who downgraded the sacraments, recalled the preaching-teaching ministry to its rightful place as a means of grace without demeaning the sacraments. We reminded one another, therefore, that Trinity's ministry should not exalt the pulpit, the altar, the church school, or the counseling chamber. Our struggle to discern the biblical image of ministry provided dynamic context for this teaching thrust on the sacraments. Sermons, lectures, and forums in the church school, conversations throughout the parish, one lecture in each series of the new members' classes, and teen-age catechetics were the means employed to teach that the sacraments—baptism and the Lord's Supper—are acts of the church instituted by Christ who, through the earthly materials, comes to every penitent person with forgiveness of sin, deliverance from evil, and eternal life. Implementing these teaching-learning situations, specific steps were taken to bring parish practice into line with biblical theology.

Honoraria for baptisms were declined. The church's ministry, we taught, does not exact payment; grace is not purchasable. Responsible stewardship undergirds the church's ministry. Our unbending practice of accepting as sponsors at baptism only those persons who were members in good standing in a major

[8] Virginia Cary Hudson, O Ye Jigs & Juleps! (New York: The Macmillan Company, 1962), p. 1.

Protestant denomination, and urging parents to serve as sponsors, evoked bewildered, angry cries throughout the parish. But the clergy's determination and the vestry's firm support were decisive. Presently, 90 percent of the children baptized at Trinity are sponsored by their parents who are themselves faithful participants in the church. The administration of baptism at a special Sunday afternoon service was surrendered, for the vestry agreed that this sacrament is particularly meaningful when administered at a regular worship service.[9]

Today, children baptized in Trinity Church continue through the nursery, the church school, the children's church with liturgy and sermonette, and "big church," entering the first year catechetical class as worshiping-learning Christians. Along the way there are reminders and helps: the clergy engage in pastoral family counseling; the minister of music visits homes and encourages participation in the children's and junior choirs; one ordained minister and a score of lay ministers evangelize and provide pastoral care for 170 children under six years of age; the department superintendents in the church school exercise pastoral care—the cradle roll superintendent visits the new mother, and the parents of children in the kindergarten receive regular reminders of their promises at baptism. Responsible Christian parents and a responsible church are agents through which the Holy Spirit nurtures the new life which God gives at baptism. The Word in preaching and teaching motivates and fashions the sense of responsibility and equips persons to exercise it.

The Lord's Supper was administered at Trinity with dignity and reverence, but two thirds of the parish received the Word

[9] An excellent brief book for laymen on baptism is Martin Marty's *Baptism* (Philadelphia: Fortress Press, 1962).

only in the sacrament.[10] Sixty percent of the members, violating the biblical and reformation traditions, ignored the Word in preaching and teaching. Our teaching, set within the context of worship and accomplished through sermons, pastoral conversations, in the new members' classes, and in teen-age catechetics, pointed up the classical interpretations of the Lord's Supper: transubstantiation—the elements actually becoming the body and blood of Christ at the moment of consecration, with the worshiper in the mass making the sacrifice to God; symbolic—the bread and wine as symbols of Christ's body and blood, with the emphasis on man's activity. The "real presence," Calvin's and Luther's teaching, emphasizes what God has done. The bread remains bread; the wine remains wine. Christ himself comes to man in and through these elements as he also comes in gospel preaching and evangelical teaching. Certainly not all the parishioners, but a majority, have been enlightened across the years. Today most members receive the living Word in preaching, teaching, and the sacraments.

As the congregation grew numerically and in its regular worship patterns, the number of communion services was increased to four on the stated Communion Sundays; and the opportunity for parishioners to receive the sacrament *every* Sunday at a stated service was provided. Allowing for illness, weekend trips, college and military service, more than fifteen hundred members in Trinity regularly receive the Word in preaching and teaching and the sacraments.

[10] Stimulating essays on the sacrament of the Lord's Supper are found in D. M. Baillie's *The Theology of the Sacraments* (New York: Charles Scribner's Sons, 1957). Also helpful are Yngve Brilioth's *Eucharistic Faith and Practice, Evangelical and Catholic* (New York: The Seabury Press, 1956) and Helmut T. Lehmann's (editor) *Meaning and Practice of the Lord's Supper* (Philadelphia: Fortress Press, 1961).

Worship

Actually, Trinity Church is most peculiarly itself when it is gathered in the corporate act of worship, every man's proper response to God's Word. In the hour of worship the great drama of salvation is reenacted with the worshipers as eager participants, loved and therefore loving, understood and therefore understanding, receiving and therefore giving. For preaching, teaching, and the sacraments; healing, evangelizing, and committee meetings; Bible study, stewardship, and parish administration are not only means whereby the Word confronts men, but equally are the means for encouraging saved sinners to worship God.

Worship at Trinity is strikingly contemporary—hundreds of families are seated together, their faces turned expectantly toward altar and pulpit, their hearts and minds responsive to God. They present a thrilling cross-section of the community: every economic and social level; every degree of education and culture; persons coming together from rickety tenements and lavish apartments, from four-room houses and eighteen-room dwellings, crossing racial lines in a spirit otherwise impossible in any community except Christ's church. They come hungrily—"Lord, where else can we go? Thou hast the words of life."

Who can comprehend the power of the healing impulse which is born anew in the hour of Christian worship—the impulse to lay at the cross one's frustrations and hurts, hostilities and fears, self-loathing and fleeting satisfactions. In Christian worship persons sick to death of their own failure, brokenhearted over the betrayals of those near and dear to them, frightened and hurt by the newfound knowledge of a killing disease, find the power to begin again, to go on, to see it through, until Christ's victory becomes their victory, too.

The church at worship also lifts with tender, strong, re-creative hands those occasional moments of poignant, peculiar awareness in every human life—the birth of a child, the union of two individuals, the death of a beloved mate—and fixes them within the structure of eternity. The world rejoices in the birth of a child; the communion of saints introduces him into life eternal. Friends wish the newlyweds well; the church binds them to each other by binding each to God. The world offers sympathy in the hour of sorrow; the church testifies to the resurrection of the body and the life everlasting. Courageous men in hours of human crises rally whole nations to sacrifice for a season; the church equips ordinary people in all seasons to pull themselves together and do their bit to keep the world from going to pieces.

So the worshipers come, conscious of the transcendent joy that is available only to Christ's gathered people feeding on the Word in preaching and sacrament. An isolated soul can scarcely remain isolated as hundreds of voices unite in singing some great hymn of faith; as the liturgist leads in the confession of sin; as a layman comes forward to read the appointed Scripture; as the preacher allows the Word to confront the worshipers with God's judgment and healing; and as hundreds of persons, having made their offering in glad response to God's grace, plead expectantly, "Create in me a clean heart," then offer prayers for the church, the state, and the world. Christ himself is present, and his people's hearts overflow with joy, peace, hope. His people are glad to be under a judgment beyond their own and rejoice in a love that will not let them go. Answering God with hymns, prayers, and offerings, they count it good to gather in the house of the Lord.

Creature-like, pastors and people go out to sin again, and know it; but, cleansed and strengthened, they also go out to render priestly service to God and man. Because they worshiped God, some witness to a friend who is indifferent toward the claims of Christ; others treasure the strength gained and draw on it in some lonely hour of temptation; and still others stand unbending in a hard controversy for Christ's sake, uncaring that they are judged unjustly by men, their consciences captive to the Word of God. In Christian worship are born the resolves to give up some hurtful affection, the insights which lay bare one's terrible bondage to sin, the courage to launch into life again.

In spite of the frustrations and failures that keep cropping up around one and in one, worshiping man sees God brooding over chaos, leading his people across new Jordans to dry land, wiping away all tears. He sees in Christ crucified God's inexhaustible love and in Christ resurrected God's mighty victory over sin and death. Only inside Christ's church does "community" really happen; only those who know they are loved by Christ can love him in return and from his love do good to friend and foe. As one goes out from penitent, expectant worship, he is empowered to be an *alter-Christus* to his neighbor; he is motivated to practice stewardship and evangelism and to engage in social action. It becomes plain in the preaching of Christ crucified that what one does with his wants, needs, abilities, and time matters immensely now. Constrained by the love of Christ, his elect get into the forefront of current battles to strip away the power of evil and lay all things at his feet now.

So with angels and archangels and all the company of heaven, Trinity parish at worship lauds and magnifies God's holy name, remembering gladly his manifold gifts of grace, reaching eagerly for his blessings, waiting confidently and working expectantly for that glorious day when every knee shall bow and tongue confess that Christ is Lord. And—as the wind blows where it will—the Holy Spirit, brooding over the congregation at worship, enables many to repent, to believe, to trust, and to take Christ's ministry into the world, going with the light that penetrates darkness, the leaven that permeates society, the salt that preserves the new life.

CHAPTER 6
LIVING TOGETHER AT TRINITY

The fundamental characteristic of the Christian life is a sharing in the ministry of the risen and ascended Lord, and this sharing must take the form of direct witness from person to person.

—W. A. VISSER 'T HOOFT

Trinity's new life—awakened by gospel preaching, enlightened by evangelical teaching, sustained by Christian worship—testifies to God's power to transform church members into witnesses. It also demonstrates that God's power to create *koinonia* is not locked away on ancient Mediterranean shores but operates persuasively among postmoderns who drive Thunderbirds and Volkswagens, finance industry and borrow from loan companies, secure families with dependable love and wound them by infidelity. The Holy Spirit is fashioning Trinity parish into a fellowship of persons who forgive and are forgiven, understand and are understood, serve and are served—a community of persons who speak God's truth in love to one another. These twice-born persons not only preach, teach, evangelize, and give beyond their means; they also help and heal one another from the resources of God's Word. Their spirit cannot be contrived; it is God's gift to those who love and serve him.

I am writing to thank the members of Trinity for their lovingkindness in my recent illness. When I found that I must undergo surgery, I came to you with my fears. Our down-to-earth talk on surgery and the discussion of the resources in the Bible helped me. When the operation was over, there were cards from friends in Trinity. My fellow teachers in the Sunday church school sent me a lovely planter. Every day, one of the pastors visited. Now I am home convalescing. My undershepherds bring each Sunday's taped sermon; our Homemaker visits and helps us weekly.

Every Man a Priest

God's grace has transformed many parishioners through the Christlike words and deeds of their concerned fellow members. One woman whose husband died unexpectedly was entertained at dinner by another widow who offered friendship and also economic help if it were needed. "I had no idea she was like that," said the first woman. "I always thought she was rather 'uppity' and cold. She's just reserved, shy, I suppose. A real friendship seems to be opening. It means so much to me."

A former vestryman who died prematurely—a reserved man not given to sentimental speech—said one afternoon from his hospital bed:

These Christian talks about death and resurrection give me strength. After all, I am dying. There's no sense in anyone pretending I'm not. My wife has meant more to me in these months than I ever realized. Her faith and love are a real support, and I know she will rear the children well. Dr. _____ (a parishioner) has been a tower of strength. He tells me straight out what I can expect and talks to me about Christ.

Another parishioner in middle life, converted to Christianity and struggling against a return to an unwholesome past, wrote:

I've had a hard life and I'm trying to do things like a Christian should. Last week _____ visited me and said she wanted me to know that she was at hand if I needed her. She understands my trouble and wants to help. Only in Trinity Church has anyone really cared about me in twenty years.

A schoolteacher and her husband, also a professional person, reported on *koinonia* in their home.

The Friday after Christmas, we had about twenty-five Trinity people here for supper and an evening of serious conversation. It was an exhilarating evening—great fun and much good talk between real persons.
1. We were "homesick" for our friends from the Family Class.
2. We wanted to entertain socially the Negroes who had joined our church.
3. We wanted new people, like the _____, to have a chance to meet others. My husband and I were sure that Trinity people would gladly accept the Negro families. But I didn't want a few guests to mar our expected good fellowship. So I decided to tell everyone by phone that these families were coming. Every person responded positively—enthusiastically, you'll be glad to know. We had an exciting evening—"existential" in every sense.

A husband steadily addressed the Word to his wife's unrealistic attitude toward death, which was destructive to the whole family, until one day the Spirit broke through with healing. "One morning, for no apparent reason," she confided, "my obsessive fear was gone. It simply isn't there anymore."

There is also the wife who helped her once irresponsible husband to become a decisive mate and responsible parent.

The anguish we have both known is over. It has proved to be a blessing in disguise. Both of us have tested God, and our experience of his forgiveness has helped us to forgive one another. And as we asked, "Why, why," we began to probe into self rather than at each other. Self-surrender is growing and with it charity and patience with each other. Suddenly, we have realized that we love each other and that we need each other and that we were meant for each other. Now we talk for hours and are really communicating.

A high school junior confronted his respectable but unchurched father so vigorously that the parent was converted to Christianity. One couple, the partners having had damaging backgrounds, were constrained by their maturing faith to engage in a series of critical pastoral conversations with the clergy and with each other. Now they are fashioning a remarkably mature Christian home. A divorcee discovered through pastoral conversations with a parent, a parishioner, and a pastor that the abundant life comes only to persons who repent and do Christ's commandments. A professional man, having passed from death into life, carries on daily pastoral conversations in his home and among his clientele. And scores of parishioners, allowing the Spirit to enlighten them concerning transient and abiding values, are pursuing a more excellent way of life. One such parishioner has written: "We may never get to the top of the corporation ladder now, but my husband is so much better in our home since he stopped pursuing 'status.' The preaching and counseling have made him so different. He is becoming a real father to the children. He's never been so happy, and that means happiness for all of us."

Homes forced to the brink of disaster by marital infidelity, severe parental irresponsibility, alcoholism, gambling, and sloth have been re-created because a wayward or weak mate was healed by God through person-to-person encounters inside the family. Penitent, possessed of new insights, enabled to love creatively, these hard-pressed families are learning firsthand what "greater good because of evil" really means. As one couple has written:

Our marriage was a sham before. Now that I see the problem, and am struggling with it, the marriage is becoming meaningful. We are discovering unsuspected depths through our personal encounters. That hymn is true—"greater good because of evil" describes our experience. It makes me shudder to think our marriage and life's meaning would have been lost to us if we hadn't been in the church and been persuaded to look at our situation in God's presence. We've been talking to some of our unchurched friends about their need for the church. I believe that God let us get into trouble to show us how life can be with him.

But human freedom—misused and disused—decrees that some gallant mates be tried and tested almost unbearably. Their unequal share of hardship makes sense only in the light of that day when God will wipe away all tears. One desperate wife wrote: "Will my husband never change? His drinking makes a shambles of our home. My mother keeps harping at me, 'Divorce him,' but I love him. He needs me. I want the strength to go on. God help me, or I'll lose my mind."

137

This ministry of cure and care by layman for layman, with some assistance from the clergy, is exercised beyond hearth and home. Many members who acknowledge God as Father are accepting one another as brothers and sisters. A very practical evidence of this creative relationship between persons is their willingness to provide employment for fellow members released from mental hospitals, private sanitoriums, and correctional institutions. This was the amazed response of one teen-ager who, having run afoul of the law, was helped by a parishioner.

I thought no one cared about what happens to me. When you called Mr. _____ to see if he could give me a job, I thought to myself, "That's for the birds; he won't care about me." When he did, I couldn't believe it. The job means more than the money. I didn't know we had people like that in our church.

One parishioner helped five of these persons whose problems were, for a season, too much for them. In spite of an embarrassing failure with one, he did not hesitate to take four more candidates for rehabilitation. Several parishioners, having had employees who handled money carelessly, declined recourse to the law and gave them the opportunity to make financial restitution and allowed them to keep their jobs. Some problem drinkers, unwilling to accept formal counseling, are helped and supported as weaker brethren.

The parish also provides money through its local benevolence budget to help economically hard-pressed members. Groceries are purchased, overdue rents are paid, modest family budgets shattered by heavy hospital bills are steadied, and the cost of psychiatric counseling is provided for persons who could not otherwise afford this care. A nonmember in the community, learning of this strand in Trinity's ministry, strengthened it with the outright gift of $3,800! Many members also assume personally a measure of support for economically distressed fellow members.

Six years ago the congregation established an education fund for its youth, enlarging it annually as a regular item in the benevolence budget. Since we are convinced that the church errs in aiding only "ministerial students," the fund is open to any member who demonstrates reasonable academic competence and shows economic need. There is no interest charge or legal requirement for repayment. A young vestryman, admissions officer at a local college, not only volunteered to administer the scholarship fund but also to counsel any high school student in the congregation interested in attending college. In this fashion, areas of pastoral care pass unobtrusively from the office of the clergy to the office of qualified laymen.

The parish views these economic expressions of concern for its members as being compatible with its present "second mile" economic support for overseas missionaries, its sponsorship of six American missions, 1959-1964, its deep involvement in social ministry in downtown Lancaster, and its consistent shattering of synodical apportionments. We are persuaded that the parish which responds generously to the needs of persons in other localities, but neglects the material and personal aspects of pastoral care in its own backyard, mutilates the church's ministry as severely as the parochial-minded congregation which declines to accept mature responsibilities beyond parish boundaries. The "foreign mission" concept alone is *not* consistent with the biblical image of the church as mission.

As Trinity Church became heterogeneous, not only did the number of members evidencing material need increase, but the walls of middle-class respectability, like the walls of Jericho, came tumbling down. As regiments of economically strained, socially insecure persons rubbed shoulders and exchanged ideas with a rising corps of aggressively "successful" and socially accepted persons, tensions and conflict have been frequent. This mass of prickly, proud humanity would have mixed like uncongenial blood types except for the Holy Spirit's creative work. Because of his labors the parishioners are learning to accept one another as persons; true community is emerging. A liberal arts graduate married to a professional man put it this way: "Only in a church like ours can I be part of a truly heterogeneous community—heterogeneous in age, racial, social, economic, and educational levels. Our children, privileged in so many other ways, rarely acquire this advantage because of our suburban location, except in Trinity Church, where we experience real community."

Members come forward from time to time expressing honest concern for fellow members whom they think are drinking too much, giving the appearance of evil, or engaging in sharp business practices. Some of these critiques reflect only a difference in social values. Stratified classes in America tend to confuse *their* mores with Christian ethics, and Trinity has *all* the strata. Some critiques, however, are relevant. The concerned layman or one of the clergy, if we think personal confrontation will be creative, meets with the parishioner in question. Many of these pastoral meetings have been constructive. The brethren are speaking God's truth in love to one another in Trinity parish.

The Holy Spirit, leveling social, economic, and cultural barriers in Trinity, is also breaching the racial barrier. A decade ago Trinity had an occasional forum on the "Negro problem" and sponsored a vacation school in concert with four other congregations, including the city's two Negro churches. That was Trinity's witness. Slowly we recognized that these occasional discussions and the two-week school were in fact "activities" which tended to insulate the parish against involvement with Negroes as *persons*. From the outset the clergy had underscored the social implications of the gospel, reminding the vestry and parishioners that God judges each Christian on his custodianship of the whole gospel. They stated periodically that they did not view their call as a special summons to integrate the races, obliterate social cleavages, or foster a particular political point of view. They understood their call as a summons to obey the Christian God who had demonstrated on Calvary that his kingdom is open to all penitent sinners, and they viewed any Christian promulgating views or acting contrary to God's purposes as being guilty of treason against his kingdom.

The racial issue, like other social issues, was discussed theologically in the vestry and throughout the parish. Sermons were preached on prejudice, fear, minority groups, and America's depersonalized life in the light of the gospel. God's judgment and grace fell where the Spirit decreed. Meanwhile, specific actions were authorized by the vestry. A teen-age canteen was opened to both races; a parish auxiliary became actively engaged in seeking job opportunities for qualified Negroes; a Boy Scout troop, interdenominational and interracial, was organized to serve the downtown neighborhood. The spirit of God, brooding over the congregation, opened many hearts and minds. Then, on Palm Sunday, five years ago, nine Negroes attended the adult classes and became confirmed members in the historic congregation where the founder of Lutheranism in America had preached the gospel of love two long centuries before!

Petulant voices were heard; some angry voices were raised.

Several dozen families "groused," drifted from church to church for a season, and finally returned to worship regularly. Only a handful transferred. Several members, arguing stridently that they would not be seated in a pew with a Negro, were reminded that any ungracious act would bring excommunication. On the other hand, hundreds of members accepted the Negroes as persons. The Negro members in turn have not been coddled or patronized; they are expected to serve Christ according to their talents. One sings in the senior choir and serves as a regular soloist for the Friday noonday service. Another served on a vestry committee. One represented the congregation at a synod-wide assembly, being the only Negro in attendance. Another taught regularly in the church school until his employment took him to another city. Here is that Negro's remembrance of Trinity Church.

Like a great many other people, we had become just a bit cynical about the Christian church in America. There was some justification for this cynicism. Too many churches are mere social clubs with boards of directors, a President, and numerous vice-presidents. Too often, they serve just one class, one race, or one economic group, and are separated from real day-to-day life.

Trinity Church is different in every sense of the word. We know because we searched and searched for the things that would support our doubt. To our delight, we discovered that it was what we had always felt a church should be—a dynamic force in an uneasy community and world. It has a heterogeneous, evangelistic membership, and clergy who, in their forthright, rugged leadership, could never be called mere caretakers.

It is not an "easy" church. It does not pat you on the head or soothe your conscience. It disturbs you, even angers you; but it also inspires you to act, if not with complete wisdom, at least with purpose and a sense of mission.

Recently, another Negro family was received into membership; the wife was invited to teach in the church school. Negro guests are frequent worshipers. Significantly, some white members are now taking specific actions in behalf of their Negro brethren on many fronts. Concerned not only about job opportunities for them, they are presently engaged in seeking to open residential Lancaster to their brethren now ghettoed in a crowded corner of the city. Several Trinity members, community leaders, exhibit responsible citizenship in these areas. Two serve on the citizen's advisory committee to the mayor; another made heavy inroads against prejudice while serving as a cabinet member in two state administrations; several are willing employers. During the summer of 1963 Lancaster's citizenry had the opportunity to sign a covenant testifying to their willingness to accept and foster integrated housing in their neighborhoods. A local newspaper reported by midsummer that a thousand persons had signed the document, three hundred and thirteen of whom were members in Trinity Church. Naturally this open declaration on integrated housing awakened negative and positive responses from our fellow citizens. Some anonymous phone calls and letters were on this order: "You damn troublemaker. I suppose you want your kid to marry a ———. Why don't you go and live in Philadelphia instead of Lancaster!" One of Trinity's more cultured critical-minded parishioners, having signed the covenant on housing, wrote encouragingly:

Trinity is a fellowship in which I live, voluntarily, my Christian ideals of racial brotherhood. Do you remember the TV show, "The Quiet Revolution"? It made the point that, although 11 A.M. Sunday may indeed be the most segregated hour of the week, it is also the

143

hour in which some people voluntarily cross racial barriers, while in other hours more people may be forced by law and circumstances to work, play, and study together. In Trinity, the sensitive conscience can hardly avoid the large and important issues of human concern, because these are vigorously presented in the light of the cross. This is any congregation's best contribution to a society scarred and bleeding from racial prejudice and class conflict.

This report does not imply—much less suggest—that Trinity Church, in concert with several other churches and the local theological seminary, has "solved" the minority problem in Lancaster. That will require a generation here, and longer in some places. But the report does present certain theoretical arguments as actual events:

1. Members of minority groups can be accepted as persons in the local parish.

2. The parish can be constrained by gospel preaching and evangelical teaching to transform many people into a real community.

3. The biblical-theological approach, rather than the sociological or political approach, is the church's proper strategy in the world.

4. Fidelity to God's Word, not results, is the primary standard of judgment.

5. Eschatology is relevant to today's decisions; Christians are convinced that it is better to fail immediately with a cause that God ordains to succeed ultimately than to succeed immediately in a cause which God marks for ultimate failure.[1]

---

[1] See Kyle Haselden, *The Racial Problem in Christian Perspective* (New York: Harper & Row, 1959), especially Part III, "The Bonds of Unity." Also James H. Burtness and John P. Kildahl, editors, *The New Community in Christ* (Minneapolis: Augsburg Publishing House, 1963).

So the Word of God in Trinity parish has awakened persons to the reality of sin, motivated some to repent, equipped them to witness in the world, and enabled them to render priestly service to one another. Parents counsel children, mates counsel mates, neighbors counsel neighbors, parishioners counsel their vestry and clergy, and the clergy and vestry counsel parishioners.

Pastoral Counseling

Prompted by the Word in preaching and teaching, Trinity's members come eagerly to their ordained shepherds for pastoral conversation. This intimate response to the Word in preaching and teaching is not unique; it is characteristic of the church's ministry across the centuries. Before Freud had produced any scientific offspring, John Watson (Ian MacLaren) was pointing up the significance of counseling in an early Lyman Beecher lecture series at Yale.

The pastor gives much of his time to consultation, and it is likely that he will have to give more every year; . . . there are times and moods and circumstances when every person desires to open his heart to some brother-man; . . . is it not good that there is within reach one ordained to be a friend unto everyone who is lonely and in distress of mind? [2]

The maturing sciences of personality have goaded, enriched, and corrected Christian insights into the nature of man. But Christian concern for persons, more evident in some periods of church history than in others, became a norm for judging authentic ministry when Jesus received Nicodemus by night and the rich young ruler by day, with each seeking "pastoral coun-

[2] John Watson, *The Cure of Souls* (New York: Dodd, Mead & Company, 1896), pp. 235-36.

seling." [3] The church where no one counsels, except the clergy, fractures Christ's ministry. "In the evangelical churches, the churches of the priesthood of all believers, anyone can become a pastoral counselor." [4] But pastoral care is not equally everybody's business. It is, however, one of the ordained minister's preeminent tasks. Viewing it in this way, Trinity's clergy called for regular office hours for all staff members, a new parish practice. Pastoral counseling by appointment began immediately.

Among the 158 persons who made and kept appointments that first year were seventeen whose emotional ills were greater than the clergy's technical skills. These were encouraged to seek specialists; pastoral *care* was continued. Among those who accepted the judgment that psychiatric counseling was needed was a young married couple on the threshold of divorce. The pastor, in consultation with the psychiatrist who treated the psychotically possessive wife, offered the resources of the Word to steady both partners. Without the counselor the couple would scarcely have sought help from the psychiatrist. Without the psychiatrist the wife's psychosis would have ruined the marriage. Without pastoral counseling a badly limping marriage may not have sustained the strains induced by psychotherapy. The marriage of psychiatry and Christian counseling will not likely occur, but psychiatrists and pastors can be partners in healing.[5]

[3] See Charles F. Kemp, *Physicians of the Soul* (New York: The Macmillan Company, 1947) and John T. McNeill, *A History of the Cure of Souls* (New York: Harper & Brothers, 1951).

[4] *A Theology of Pastoral Care*, p. 334.

[5] See *Psychiatry and Religion: Some Steps Toward Mutual Understanding and Usefulness* (Report No. 48, December, 1960), formulated by the committee on psychiatry and religion. Group for the Advancement of Psychiatry, Publication Office, 104 East 25th Street, New York 10, New York; pp. 317-64. Also Granger E. Westberg, *Minister and Doctor Meet* (New York: Harper & Row, 1961).

The demand for pastoral counseling which began as a rivulet became a swollen flood. By 1957 there were fifty or so appointments each month focused primarily at that time in the office of the senior pastor. It was an onerous burden.[6] Having reached the conviction that the ordained minister who "specializes" fragments the ministry of Christ, the pastor felt himself caught in a vise between theory and practice. The vestry and clergy, orienting to the biblical image of ministry and wrestling with the demands of a rapidly changing parish situation, made these decisions:

1. A lay assistant was called to share in administration, evangelism, stewardship, and youth work. 2. The senior pastor faced up to the truth that he was caricaturing the biblical image of ministry—he was becoming the *counselor*. 3. The staff directed many nonmembers to competent community counseling services. 4. The vestry and clergy joined with representative clergy, doctors, and lawyers in the community to establish a pastoral counseling center under the auspices of the local council of churches. Counseling appointments at Trinity still run to forty a month; a third are now handled by three other staff members.

Our experience demonstrates that where people respond to gospel preaching, seek evangelical teaching, and receive Christ in the sacraments—where they discover that they are accepted, understood, and cared for as persons and their confidences kept —the counseling calendar is crowded.[7] We are not disposed to

[6] See Russell L. Dick's "Finding Time for Counseling," in *The Minister's Consultation Clinic*, edited by S. Doniger (New York: Channel Press, 1955).

[7] See Seward Hiltner, *Preface to Pastoral Theology* (Nashville: Abingdon Press, 1958) and *The Christian Shepherd* (Nashville: Abingdon Press, 1959); William E. Hulme, *Counseling and Theology* (Philadelphia: Fortress Press, 1956)—especially Chapters 1, 3, 6, 8, and 9; Carroll A. Wise, *Pastoral Counseling, Its Theory and Practice* (New York: Harper & Row, 1951); and Thurneysen's *A Theology of Pastoral Care*, pp. 200-252.

reveal the breadth and depth of pastoral counseling at Trinity, for this is the story of flesh-and-blood persons in an identified parish. But hints of *koinonia* can be caught in this cursory sketch.

Premarital counseling is required before the clergy perform any marriage in Trinity Church. The number of sessions vary from one to eight, depending on age, background, mutuality, emotional maturity, and Christian commitment. Multiple problems are presented in these counseling sessions: emotional unreadiness for marriage, pregnancy, economic inadequacy, escape from unpleasant parental situations, garbled information on sex and widespread experimentation but little understanding of it in relation to love and marriage, domination of one person by another, severe differences in values, incipient conflict with prospective in-laws, basic differences in religious traditions and convictions, and occasionally, evidences of psychotic behavior in one partner, or sometimes both, resulting in negative mutuality.

A startling number of teen-agers experiment with sex these days. This teen-age promiscuity, reflecting as well as contributing to a relativistic morality, is not uncommon among youth from church homes. Parents often ask, "What did we do wrong?" There may be several answers: over-parenting which sows the seeds of rebellion in strong-minded children, under-parenting which denies youth a moral frame of reference for responsible decision making, and human freedom and temperament which points up the dreadful implications of this freedom. A fourth pattern seems to be emerging. Some teen-agers point the shot gun at their parents; the pregnancy is not an "accident."

In these complex situations the young couple and both sets of parents are invited to share in the pastoral conversations.

Confronted by God's judgment and grace, encouraged to exercise their freedom responsibly, the young people respond in various ways: A few surrender the child for adoption, not as an escape from reality but sacrificially in what they consider to be the interests of the child; some accept the child and rear him out of wedlock, occasionally making an honest marriage with someone else in later years; some, overwhelmed by their undisciplined love, repent, accept forgiveness from God, parents, and one another, and marry, claiming God's boundless grace; a few reject pastoral conversations after one meeting. The majority look to the Word as the best resource for transmuting pain into growth, weakness into strength.

Before a ceremony is performed for any teen-agers, it is agreed that the couple will seek further counseling if any problem—in-laws, money, child-rearing, marital relations—is unresolved after a month's open discussion between the partners. Many are back in the counselor's office within a year. Some are helped; others are not. The latter add to the mounting national statistics which prove that few teen-agers, even under the most hospitable circumstances, are ready for marriage.

We are also concerned that older, more mature couples exhibit mutuality. Discerning no evidence of mutual faith, values, and ideals, Trinity's clergy ordinarily decline to perform the ceremony, putting forth their observations and reasons. If, for example, the couple cannot resolve their religious differences through counseling prior to marriage, we consider it unlikely that they will resolve them after the ceremony. If one "gives in" or both drift into secular living after marriage, the church considers those "solutions" to be unacceptable.[8] Each couple is

---

[8] James A. Pike's *If You Marry Outside Your Faith* (Rev. ed.; New York: Harper & Row, 1962) is a sound, practical study to share with these counselees.

guided in examining the social, cultural, physical, "political"—two-family backgrounds—and spiritual implications of their proposed union. During these discussions interpersonal reactions and interactions between the man and woman open fresh teaching-counseling opportunities. A basis is laid for the couple's realistic recognition of some continuing differences and their creative handling of them.

Marriage counseling constitutes half the counseling appointments at Trinity. Pastoral marriage counseling is not directed toward saving a particular marriage, but toward helping both partners bring themselves under God's judgment and grace so that each may perceive reality, accept it, and decide to work through personal and communal problems creatively. Lancaster and Trinity Church buttress the sociologists' reports on the American home in flux: here, too, families are exhibiting an inability to handle economic affluence; parental authority is shaken; morality is considered to be relativistic; there is an existential concern that civilization may be obliterated in a nuclear holocaust. These complex, dynamic forces are at work everywhere disorganizing and reorganizing the American family. It is not evident presently whether these changes will strengthen or destroy the institutions of marriage and family as we have previously known them. Pastoral counseling with hundreds of American families convinces me that fully one quarter of all married couples are critically unhappy and that perhaps 20 percent of the marriages are in name only, for the emotional isolation of the partners is total.[9] David and Vera Mace report

[9] To suggest that half the American homes are emotionally unstable may be conservative. More divorces are granted annually in the United States than in the rest of the world combined. See James H. S. Bossard, "Divorce, Some Selected Repercussions," in *Man and Wife*, edited by E. H. Mudd and A. M. Krich (New York: W. W. Norton & Company, 1957).

that one-half of America's married couples are living unhappily with each other.[10]

Consequently, we are confronted with a welter of human needs in marriage and family counseling. There are mature marriages where one or both partners, awakened by the gospel, suspect that there are new dimensions of excellence to be realized in their marriage. There are homes where husband-wife relationships are wholesome, but parental relationships are limping. Some teen-agers, also awakened by the gospel, seek help in self-understanding when their parents cannot or will not provide it. Most of our marriage counseling, however, has to do with couples whose marriages are strained by tensions caused by unwholesome relationships with in-laws, too much as well as too little money, alcohol, conflicting social interests, cultural differences, and colliding religious beliefs. We are also confronted by marriages marred by infidelity, hostility, boredom, and by marriages in which both partners, determined on divorce, are referred by a concerned lawyer who thinks the marriage can be saved. Where sexual maladjustment, acute or chronic, frustrates a marriage, the counselor usually finds this to be symptomatic of deeper emotional conflicts in one or both partners. Persons victimized by *any* deep-seated neurosis or psychosis are referred to a psychiatrist in private practice or to a community agency equipped to provide depth counseling. Ten percent of those who first seek our service are referred to specialists. Others we often can help:

For several years my wife and I have discussed our need for marriage counseling. Both of us were hesitant. We decided our need was

---

[10] David R. and Vera Mace, *Marriage: East and West* (New York: Doubleday & Company, 1960).

not severe enough to justify our coming. But during the discussion on Hiltner's *Self-Understanding* we decided differently.

We are not forty yet, but suddenly we see the empty places waiting for us when the last child is reared. We aren't prepared to live without them. We talk to each other pleasantly, but except for the children we don't communicate at all. I don't know her as a person, and she doesn't know me. She agreed that I should make an appointment. We find it difficult to take this step. I talked it over with _____, whom you counseled several years ago.

"Personal problem" counseling contributes to Trinity's crowded appointment calendar. Here too we meet multiple human needs: interfamily, two generation conflicts; feelings of inferiority; anxiety neuroses; deception in business; petty theft; alcoholism; social drinking; bitter, recurring attacks on mate, parent, or friend; gambling; social or religious prejudice; premarital relations; false witness; pregnancy before marriage; homosexuality; frustration; job failure; academic failure in high school and college—teen-agers often suffer more acutely from personal failure than older persons; guilt, real and imagined.[11] With few exceptions homosexuals and alcoholics are referred to specialists.

Some problems can be resolved in several sessions. Most, however, are symptomatic of deep emotional conflict. The preaching of God's judgment and grace motivates many people to tackle their personal problems; and some, counseled and shepherded into a meaningful relationship with God, gain improved emotional and mental health, as this letter witnesses:

[11] The pastoral counselor has a significant contribution to make in a culture where guilt and redemption are strangely separated. See Lewis J. Sherrill, *Guilt and Redemption* (Rev. ed.; Richmond: John Knox Press, 1957) and Paul Tournier, *Guilt and Grace* (New York: Harper & Row, 1962).

My husband has accepted a new position, and we are presently en-route to ———————. It was with deep regret that we left Lancaster. This past summer was filled with problems and heartaches for us, and it was only our Christian faith and the counseling which helped us to make some realistic and difficult decisions. Trinity Church was the keystone in our happiness in Lancaster.

Vocational counseling falls equally to the whole professional staff. Three quarters of the clientele are between fifteen and twenty-five years of age. During the second year of catechetical instruction the clergy discuss with the youth vocation, sex, dating, courtship, and marriage. The ensuing pastoral conversations are extended to include any parents who also seek guidance. We encourage parental cooperation with the vocational and guidance counselors in the city and township schools. Community agencies, the testing center at Franklin and Marshall College, and other specific resources are also employed. Young men who give strong evidence of being emotionally healthy, spiritually sensitive, intellectually curious, decisive in temperament, and socially at ease with both sexes are encouraged to give critical, prayerful consideration to the full-time ministry as one Christian vocation among many. All youth, however, are encouraged to consider a career for which they appear to be providentially endowed. Marriage is presented as a Christian vocation to be entered into seriously, reverently, permanently.

We also meet a number of persons thirty to sixty years of age whose main problem is job adjustment. Occasionally, one makes a radical change in vocation. Most, however, find through pastoral counseling the insight and motivation to go on constructively, sometimes creatively, where they are.

Trinity's staff is aware of no member in the parish who, wanting it, has escaped pastoral conversation—the Word in person-to-person encounter—with the clergy or a fellow member. Not all have responded by any means, but none has been altogether neglected. The fact that 60 percent of the present membership have voluntarily made and kept formal counseling appointments with a professional staff member testifies to the parishioners' confidence in pastoral counseling.

The foregoing presentation is necessarily superficial, perfunctory; for we are dealing with identifiable persons in an identified parish. But the sensitive, imaginative reader will catch in this sketch some hints of *koinonia* in a parish where people *are* learning to live together creatively through their personal encounters with God's Word.

Additional evidences of *koinonia* can be discerned in the tensions which swirl around the pastoral counselor. First, there is tension when a young couple—wholesomely in love, evidencing emotional health, and holding faith, values, and background in common—is harassed by a neurotic parent who, objecting to the proposed marriage, urges the pastoral counselor to discourage it. He, in turn, seeks to get both generations together before the marriage is solemnized. He seeks to guide all the parties toward recognizing and accepting reality. He counsels the couple to be understanding and patient with their parents without being dominated by them; he performs the ceremony. But the tensions are often severe for the couple and the counselor. The following case history, written by a former member now living in a distant city, could have been written by three-score counselees.

When I first sought counseling help, I was at the point of distraction from a running battle of several years with my parents' efforts to block my marriage. From counseling I gained the spiritual guidance not only to analyze my person and my situation, but the courage to cope with it—and that growth was painful. Through pastoral counseling I learned how to recognize and handle my family's neurotic demands, to recognize my neurotic responses, and to get free of some, while at the same time coming to peace of mind in the conviction that I was doing right in God's sight. Through counseling I started toward emotional stability and spiritual maturity which have helped to make a solid foundation for our marriage and family life.

My husband, who participated in the final personal counseling sessions and all the premarital sessions with me, says that the counseling first saved me from a nervous breakdown and then set me on the road to making a real marriage. He also says that preaching is important, but that it is in the shaping of human relationships through counseling from God's Word that a pastor best emulates the Carpenter of Nazareth.

Second, tensions develop when the counselor, after several interviews, declines to perform a particular marriage. Significantly, seventeen couples denied marriage in Trinity Church and married elsewhere have returned for marital counseling. On the other hand, fifty-three couples, denied marriage in Trinity, proceeded to marry elsewhere and have not sought our counseling service. A number of these marriages, to one's knowledge, have ended in divorce. What happened to the others? (1) The counselor's judgment was in error. (2) The couple, getting into marital difficulties, sought counseling elsewhere. (3) Like many married couples in our faceless generation, they are settling for a drab marriage of convenience which runs the risk of unfaithfulness by one or both partners. (4) The time is limited; any one of the foregoing possibilities may be realized. This does not imply that premarital counseling at Trinity exudes an aura of magic. Some marriages approved and performed by our clergy during the decade have also ended in divorce. On the other hand, many marriages have been strengthened, and many persons have been challenged to view this vocation with new seriousness. "Marryin' Sam" finds no place on Trinity's staff.

Third, tensions are engendered occasionally when the clergy marry divorced persons. Some church people cannot and others will not adjust to the evangelical counselor's frame of reference for counseling *all* who come forward and thereafter marrying *some*. But the shepherd-prophet will not close the door on any human need simply to protect himself from criticism or to avoid possible mistakes in pastoral judgment. The counselor and the counselee must find their way from the resources of the Word. Each situation is different. Christ's ministry is prostituted where *all* divorced persons are rejected mechanically, or married indiscriminately.

Fourth, tensions *can* spill from the counseling chamber into the worship hour. Occasionally a counselee will apply parts of a sermon to his confused person. If, however, the pastoral counselor refers psychotic and severely neurotic persons to the psychiatrist, and if his relationship is deeply *pastoral,* these situations occur infrequently. Ordinarily, *pastoral* counselees are not excused from God's demands, and those who are helped by psychiatrists must eventually come under the demands of the gospel. Personal adjustment and salvation cannot be equated. The pastoral counselor, accepting persons as they are, does not offer "cheap grace."

Fifth, tensions can arise between the pastoral counselor and the psychiatrist, social worker, or family doctor. It is the mutual responsibility of these helping-healing professions, validating their concern for persons, to make these tensions creative. Recognizing the need for dialogue between the helping-healing disciplines not only in national and regional conferences but also in thousands of American communities, a group of Lancaster clergy, psychiatrists, social workers, and physicians present points of view, examine techniques, and engage in dialogue at monthly luncheon meetings. Regularly, we wrestle not only with our pride but also with our dogma—scientific or religious—so that we do not hurt whom we seek to help.

The scientific counselor is an indispensable helper and, at many levels, a partial healer. But he cannot reconcile anyone to God. This is the work of Christ. The scientific counselor can offer help to persons who plead as Macbeth did:

> Canst thou not minister to a mind diseas'd,
> Pluck from the memory a rooted sorrow,
> Raze out the written troubles of the brain,
> And with some sweet oblivious antidote
> Cleanse the stuff'd bosom of that perilous stuff
> Which weighs upon the heart?

But the pastoral counselor knows that God, not man, blots out sin "as far as the east is from the west." The skills of the pastoral counselor are means for bringing Christ to troubled minds and anguished hearts. God heals. Participating in the church's ministry, the counselor is the mediator of God's judgment and grace; he does not view spiritual healing and psychological adjustment as interchangeable experiences. And he takes Christ's love to persons to whom healing has not come, if they will have him.

The Context for Pastoral Conversation

Although counseling can occur, effective or not, between willing persons anywhere, pastoral counseling cannot occur outside *koinonia.* The parish pastor who counsels extensively and intensively is in a precarious position which at first glance seems to preclude effective counseling. He lives with three hundred or three thousand persons in multiple, complex, uncertain relationships. His interpersonal relationships with fellow workers, professional and volunteer, are under close scrutiny. As the administrative officer of the corporation, he leads in making some unpopular decisions and accepts executive responsibility for vestry decisions which are rarely unanimous or unanimously endorsed in the parish. His family relationships are scrutinized, discussed, evaluated; his salary and living situation concern some, especially those who contribute the least. His leadership in the community is subject to continual appraisal. He receives far too much adulation and is subjected occasionally to vicious criticism. A sensitive conscience tempts him to become involved in social, economic, and political reforms to the neglect of the more exasperating business of confronting persons with God's Word. And human nature—not least his own—is bent so stubbornly against God that defeat piled on defeat riddles the strongest ministry. Nonetheless, he is under orders to speak and do God's truth which judges before it heals. The parish pastor certainly needs self-understanding. Even more he needs to experience God's judgment and grace daily.

No one can assess the amount of harm which well-intentioned ministers have done through lack of understanding of their own psychological needs, hostilities, and fears; but on any fair view it is quite considerable. Let us put the same point positively. When the minister has begun to be released from false pretenses, from unacknowledged anxieties, and is learning the joy of entering freely into the comradeship of the search for the meaning of life with another person, the high potentialities for his becoming a channel of grace may be realized. . . . The constructively healthy personalities have for the most part known radical inner struggle. We are not asking for personalities neatly grooved. We are asking only how the struggles we have may lead to constructive understanding rather than to despair.[12]

The pastoral counselor, like any other counselor, needs emotional health. He also needs the daily correction of his insights and the purification of his motives in the fires of evangelical faith, and the recognition and acceptance of *his* need to be understood, forgiven, loved. Pastoral counseling, a function of the church's ministry, does not occur outside *koinonia*. This is inescapably plain when the counselor and counselee face up to counseling failures.

All responsible helpers and healers know the awful tensions stemming from failures which root in their own imperfect persons. One has little knowledge of the medical doctors' concern over failures tied to their personal and professional inadequacies. In a culture where legal suits over malpractice frequently reflect the irresponsible efforts of ill-intentioned, ill-advised patients to win a fast dollar, how can any doctor talk openly about his failures? It appears, however, that pastoral counselors, psychiatrists, and social workers are more open about their professional failures than medical practitioners dare to be. Legal responsibility for incompetent counseling is much harder to determine, although here too the number of suits is multiplying. But there are deeper reasons for this larger openness among counselors. Occupied with their patients' emotional and mental health, they are situationally reminded of their own limited personhood. And pastoral counselors, constrained by Christ's love, are particularly concerned about their growth as persons.

[12] Daniel D. Williams, *The Minister and the Care of Souls*, (New York: Harper & Row, 1961), p. 101.

The disciplines of pastoral counselors also differ in another basic sense. Ordinarily, an appendectomy or tonsillectomy is a routine affair; complications are rare. But no counseling situation is ever routine; human freedom and imperfections in the counselee and the counselor make the outcome of each problematical. The counselor will not brood over failures which belong on the counselee's doorstep, although he weeps for stubborn persons who resist insights or reject outright the help which could improve their emotional health. Some failures, however, do belong on the counselor's doorstep. The Christian counselor admits to them and hopes for understanding and forgiveness, and occasionally suggests another counselor. Meanwhile, he must live with the persons whom he has failed. Most of them forgive him and, conscious of human limitations in themselves, accept him as an imperfect but wholesomely motivated human being.

But what of those who do not forgive him? He catches a cynical eye as he preaches; he takes a reluctant hand at the close of the service; he works with them in parish affairs and community enterprises—aware that some consider him a pious fraud. He prays for them and for himself—and goes on with the Lord's work. All counselors have their share of failure. When the psychiatrist makes a mistake in judgment, or the medical doctor diagnoses too hurriedly, or the surgeon shrinks from bold surgery, these practitioners are not required to live closely with the persons whom they have failed. It is possible for them to get far from the knowledge of their professional mistakes and personal inadequacies—if they want it so. Not the parish pastor! Living daily with God's demands and promises and with the persons God committed to his pastoral care, he has no avenue of escape.

Koinonia makes creative life possible: he not only forgives—he is forgiven; he not only helps—he is helped; he not only understands—he is understood; he not only counsels—he is counseled. He is confronted daily by the abyss between his finite mind and the infinite mind of God, the chasm between his deep-seated ignorance and the illuminating truth that is in Christ, the gulf between his ambivalent character and the consistent character of God. The pastoral counselor does not excuse his counseling failures by recounting the high percentage of counseling successes, as though they were his and not God's. And when the tensions become unbearable, he seeks a secluded corner in his too-busy world to plead for God's forgiveness, "O wretched man that I am"; and, rising cleansed, he returns to serve, remembering how marvelously Christ used another penitent bungler, Simon Peter, to upbuild the people of God.

The Word in persuasive preaching, relevant teaching, and decisive lay witnessing prompts a steady stream of contemporary Nicodemuses, rich young rulers, and Mary Magdalenes to seek help. And the counselor, ordained or lay, is maturing as a Christian person when he—overwhelmed at being sought, his Christian insights valued—throws himself on the divine mercy, confident that he can be used by God to rescue some lost souls, and where he cannot, cares for them from Christ's love.

Pastoral care in Trinity is both spontaneous and ordered. Human needs are uncovered, diagnosed, and addressed from the resources of God's Word:

I wish I could express how much we here at the [local home for aging ladies] appreciate Trinity's kindness to us not only at the Christmas season but through the entire year. We look forward weekly to listening to the tape recording of our helpful, beautiful services at Trinity Church, and a number of other ladies here always join us. It is so kind of Mr. _____ who brings the tape recorder every week.

The regular visits from the ladies each month make us feel very much a part of the congregation. The regular visits of our ministers, and their faithfulness, make us feel secure.

Occasionally, persons are bitter in their criticism of the church's ministry because it failed them. Some criticisms are unfair; others are not. When we discover that a hard-pressed person was neglected, we do not excuse ourselves by arguing that people call the doctor, report trouble with utilities, phone the police, or turn in a fire alarm, but expect the clergy to operate from a crystal ball. We try instead to strengthen our lay and ordained shepherding procedures and skills. The biblical image of ministry haunts us. God's love constrains us to go out of our way to bring the frightened and fainthearted, the lost and lonely, the rebellious and embittered to him. But in their freedom some persons do not respond. Some soil produces no yield. Some people prefer darkness to light. Authentic ministry is proved not solely by its results, but also by its faithful sowing of the Word, its disciplined willingness to bear the light.

Trinity's members are learning to live together as God's people; they are rendering priestly service to one another and in the world. These many splendored human relationships cannot be packaged at denominational headquarters, energized by live-wire clergy, sparked by a weekend retreat at Camp Granada, or generated by hearty greeters in the friendly church. *Koinonia* is a noun; it means Christian fellowship. It is born of the Spirit wherever the Word confronts persons in their freedom, and some respond. Because this is happening in Trinity parish, *koinonia* is emerging. *Koinonia* is not a Bible study group. It is not an evangelism committee. It is not a prayer cell. *Koinonia* is two or three persons, or several thousand or ten million, who, motivated by and equipped from God's Word and obedient to it,

162

are rendering priestly service to God and man in many places, in many ways, openly and secretly. This is the New Testament image.

But man is not a disembodied spirit. He lives in a particular moment in an identifiable locality. So too does Christ's church. His Spirit-filled ministry employs institutional forms for its expression. How Trinity employs those forms is the theme of the next chapter.

CHAPTER 7

ORDER FOR THE SAKE OF FREEDOM

The principle of morality is that we should behave as Persons who are members of a Society of Persons—a Society into which Personality is itself a valid claim of entrance. —WILLIAM TEMPLE

Trinity parish learned in the agonizing process of renewal that a Spirit-filled ministry requires institutional forms. If, as Halford Luccock once observed, a sermon can splatter gelatinously around the walls of the sanctuary for want of a skeletal outline, so too can a parish, lacking sound institutional forms, dissipate the Spirit's work. But this generation of clergy at Trinity, too zealous at times in stripping away traditions, had to learn that. Fortunately, the lay leaders were stubborn teachers. Colliding initially, we agreed to examine the church in history and to re-examine the doctrinal implications of the incarnation. This is what we learned, accepted, and oriented to, with clerical and lay views being modified in the process.

From the beginning the Christian church fashioned evangelical forms to embrace and care for persons in the community, preserve apostolic truth, and carry the gospel into the world. The church's historic creeds and doctrine of the incarnation were fashioned in part to refute the docetic view of Christ which makes him less than human and robs him of historical relevance. Christianity has been able to bridge the centuries by providing a Spirit-inhabited institution through which the Word could become flesh in every generation. The historical Jesus, a child of his times, did not envision the Industrial Revolution, "the garbled lexicon of quantum physics," or orbital flights. His church, however, has lived to see all these and more; and led by his Spirit it shapes historical forms through which he can confront persons in time, forms within which it can *be* and through which it can accomplish God's mission. The sixteenth-century Reformation was, in part, a criticism of the institutionalized Christianity developed during the Middle Ages, but the reformers did not escape institutionalism. Christianity, we concluded, must bring its institutional forms under God's searching judgment to discern whether they are means or ends, but it does not disdain institutional forms as necessary means. Consequently, Trinity's parish leaders sought to preserve old forms and fashion new ones so that the parish could better exercise Christ's ministry.

The vestry no longer exalts the office of the administrator; neither does it neglect the "business" of the parish. But the clergy and lay leaders, while viewing careless administration as the sin of sloth, now consider any neglect in preaching and teaching the judgment and grace of God to be insurrection against his kingdom. The first is a vice; the second is treason. The organizational wheels still turn smoothly at Trinity. The almost unbroken set of parochial records from Colonial days has been kept as precisely during the last decade as in previous decades. Detailed annual parish reports are prepared meticulously. The treasurer's financial reports are mimeographed for monthly distribution to the vestry; each professional staff member also reports monthly. Benevolence money is remitted monthly to the synod. Parish benevolence money, used in the interests of local persons, is recorded precisely. The vestry strives for a well-ordered parish, not because they delight in tending the institution, but because effective administration frees persons to communicate the gospel.

Shaping the Worship Services

At the outset the vestry examined Trinity's traditional worship forms and patterns. Changes were agreed upon and instituted. The children's, junior, and youth choirs, previously called for on special occasions, were brought into the eleven o'clock service on rotation and, with the institution of the 8:45 service, used similarly there; worship as families was encouraged. The liturgy was explained and demonstrated at several worship services and regularly in the new members' class; congregational singing was encouraged; and the ushers, instructed, became part of each service. Sunday evenings were given to the youth and, once each month, to the adult Bible study hour, and later to other teaching ventures. The number of services on stated Communion Sundays was increased to four, and eventually the administration of the Lord's Supper was provided weekly at a third stated service. The sacrament of baptism was given a place in congregational worship. Another traditional service at Trinity was the four o'clock "quiet service" on Friday afternoons during Lent. Instituted years before by a pastor alert to reaching a rural community at the Friday farmers' markets, it was attended in 1952 by a handful of elderly folk. This service, now conducted at noonday (12:25 P.M.) and eventually expanded to a weekly pattern, September through May, is strongly attended. Presently, Trinity Church offers 220 opportunities for public worship on weekdays and Sundays; the sanctuary and chapel are open seven days a week for meditation and prayer.

Each of the four weekly worship services differs liturgically from the others. The historic liturgy is used at the eleven o'clock service: the congregation kneels for confession; the introits are sung; different musical settings are employed on festival occasions. The 8:45 service is less formal—versicles, psalm, scripture, creed, sermon, offering, prayer, and hymns. Vested choirs participate in both services. A choirmaster who is a churchman and choristers, who view themselves as ministers of the Word through sacred music, enrich the corporate worship of God. The clergy vest in cassock, surplice, and stole. Laymen, coming forward to read the appointed scripture lessons, are not vested. Vestrymen, assisting at Communion, wear the Geneva gown. The 8 A.M. Communion services are without music; the clergy wear clerical garb. The Friday noon services are plain: invocation, prayer, music, sermon, and benediction. The organist, soloist, and preacher appear in secular dress.

Laymen participate in most of the services at Trinity. They also preach occasionally at the Friday noon and Sunday services. Of course, this lay participation in the services initially disturbed some people. One of the older members wrote: "We protest the use of lay readers at our beautiful Trinity Church services. We pay you clergy to do that. And another thing I don't like is vestrymen helping at Communion. Only the ministers are supposed to be in the chancel. Nothing is the same as it used to be."

Trinity's parish leaders have also struggled to fashion worship forms which are meaningful to persons *now*. There are varieties of Christian experience; the Bible bristles with them. There are varieties of liturgical forms; Christian history is crammed with them. We teach that no single liturgy is suitable to everyone's worship experience, that man's response to the Word in preaching and teaching and the sacraments *is* Christian worship, that a liturgy which is relevant today—simple or rich, traditional or newly fashioned—may be archaic next year, and that forms which were meaningful in the sixteenth century can be excitingly relevant for some Christians today. The issue, as we see it, is not either-or, but both-and. We acted on that judgment. The parish provides not only multiple services, including weekday services, but varied liturgical forms which help postmodern man to worship God. This evaluation by a parishioner puts it in a nutshell:

Lutherans have a healthy respect for words and for the Word. Trinity does not neglect the expression of truth in liturgy, in art, or in music. Nonverbal language conveys knowledge too, often beyond our conscious reason. Wish I could remember precisely what Margaret Mead wrote (but I can't) about the importance of ritual in the development of young people—a sense of responsibility, maturity, belonging. There is a variation of this theme in the book I recently gave you, *Man's Need and God's Action*. Episcopalians, of course, have this insight profoundly. When it's good, it's very, very good. When it's bad, it's hocus-pocus, meaningless mechanics. It certainly isn't hocus-pocus at Trinity.

Electing the Official Board

If worship forms are crucial, the election of an official board is critical. Trinity's vestry was once a self-perpetuating board. The parish in 1952 was isolated from its leaders. Both the vestry and the congregation bid for the clergy's unqualified support. The clergy—convinced that the church's ordained leaders are called to bring God's Word to bear on persons, rather than to lead a parishioners' revolt or allow themselves to be taken captive by a "power elite"—called the vestry's procedures and the congregation's spectatorism before the tribunal of biblical evidence. Recognizing publicly that vestry procedures were faulty and that the constitution required amendment, the clergy maintained that the vestry could be motivated to change, and declined to discuss the board members with parishioners. The oligarchy came under the Word in the privacy of the vestry meetings; the congregation was not privy to those confrontations.

And the Word quickened and gave new life. Eventually, the vestrymen decided to amend Trinity's 1769 constitution—limited terms, rotation, lower voting age, no discrimination against sex or color, elimination of a restrictive "no debt" clause—and to nominate persons for the official board on the basis of demonstrated churchmanship. During those years of transformation the Spirit also motivated the congregation to understand their vestry's valiant efforts to become flexible in administering the parish as an instrument of Christ's ministry. But this transformation would not have occurred if the clergy and several lay cronies had rushed precipitously into conflict on secondary fronts, engaging in personal vendettas, and shaking up the parish stalwarts simply as a contest of human wills. Effecting change for the sake of change brings hurt without healing. But the biblical image is also fractured by clergy who teach doctrine and talk sonorously about the church as mission without taking clear-cut positions under constraint of the Word. This is painful to clergy and laity alike, but it is the pain of healing. In our efforts to break the impasse between theology and activism we learned that there is no magic in theology. The key is conversion. Being and doing are the existential context for communicating the Word to persons.

The present procedure for nominating and electing vestrymen is dynamic. Every member, eighteen-years-old and in good and regular standing, is encouraged to submit annually the names of candidates for the official board. Thereafter, at a regular vestry meeting the parish roll is read, each vestryman suggesting additional names. The names submitted from the congregation and suggested by the vestry are placed on a blackboard, providing the potential nominee enjoys a reputation of good report in the community and—as we have come to view all elected and appointed personnel—worships regularly, is maturing in his practice of stewardship, evangelizes, gives evidence of an emotional maturity which enables him to represent the whole congregation, and views the parish as existing to exercise Christ's ministry. From the sixty to eighty potential candidates, male and female, two nominees are presented for each office. Biographical sketches of the nominees are distributed to the congregation several weeks prior to the election. Balloting is done on a Sunday morning; the polls are open from 8 A.M. until 12:30 P.M.

The result of this procedure is a vestry which exhibits a measure of Christian maturity, a sense of personal responsibility, a readiness to grow theologically, and a decisive temper of mind. Talented, responsible, knowledgeable in the faith, they are prickly on occasion, the endurable price of creative thinking.

Without the capacity and disposition to handle creative ideas and the ensuing conflicts without pettiness, parish renewal may not have happened. This transformation of the vestry, however, came through the transformation of its personnel. No one was voted out or crowded out. The men decided to alter the face of Trinity's governing board.

The vestry is comprised of twenty-one elected laymen; the clergy also attend, having voice and vote. A vestryman may serve two consecutive terms. It is not rotation, however, but the procedure on and requirements for nomination which allow us to call forward persons who can face the pressures of leadership. Naturally, a few members decline to serve because "too much" is expected of them, but the majority take satisfaction in being called to responsible places of leadership. The standing committees, chaired by vestrymen and members of the congregation, function primarily because they are staffed with individuals of initiative, judgment, and courage who, given the freedom to function, know that they are expected to function and are capable of doing so. Once advisable, the clergy's attendance at all committee meetings is no longer necessary.

All matters of human judgment are settled by majority vote. On the other hand, basic biblical and theological affirmations, such as the equality of persons before God, are not subject to a vote in the vestry or congregation. It is treason against the King to discuss, debate, table, or disdain what God has decided. Congregations with this kind of leadership are irrelevant to society and destructive to the personhood of those who belong to them; they insulate the members against the reality of God.

The vestry's contributions would fill a book. Administratively, they stood back of the decision to construct an immense parish house at the heart of the city and have shared its facilities generously with the community. They have called ordained and lay associates to strengthen the ministry of the Word, and have provided adequate secretarial help, purchased additional downtown properties for future expansion, dealt responsibly and imaginatively with their present facilities—far too much to enumerate here. But more significantly, they have come to see themselves as Christ's ministers—overseers of his church. During these latter years when Negroes were received into membership, "second mile benevolence" was called for, the tempo of evangelistic work was increased, vestry assistants at Communion were asked for, weekly noonday services were instituted, and the replacement of our four-manual organ became pressing, the vestry supported and fostered each venture as responsible stewards should. It is, however, their exercise of Christ's ministry as lay preachers, teachers, counselors, and evangelists which testifies best to their conversion and provides the Christian basis for their leadership in Christ's church. Today every vestryman is exercising at least one function of ministry; some are exercising several; three are teachers, preachers, counselors, and evangelists.

We are not implying that *all* vestrymen from the very beginning in 1952 searched the Scriptures, entered heartily into the dialogues, discerned the biblical image of ministry, and finally accepted that image themselves. Several older men held themselves aloof from those "messy," sometimes noisy, often painful dialogues. Several were negative throughout. And one aging vestryman managed complete insulation against the new concept of ministry by falling fast asleep each time a vestry meeting was called to order! But seventeen of the initial twenty-one vestrymen eventually got involved in Christ's ministry. This response, written in 1962 by a vestryman, became characteristic: "I feel that if Trinity's 'professional' ministry is interrupted, the community will suffer an even greater loss than the congregation itself, for Trinity's lay ministry is under way. Biblical ministry is now rooted firmly in this congregation."

Trinity parish responded to the call to exercise Christ's ministry partly because its clergy and official board engaged in it themselves. The problem of the unconverted parish is too complex to be altered by the administrative skill of any bishop or synodical president. It is too complex to be resolved by ecclesiastical pronouncements, dented by pulpit oratory, or solved by prayer groups. It is too deep-rooted to be touched by theoretical statements on the nature and purpose of the church or to be affected radically by techniques, methods, and programs. Parish renewal is spiritual, theological, psychological. Clergy and laity must find an authentic image of ministry, lay hold on divine resources to enact it, and begin. Every parish pastor must wrestle with the question: "Do I want the parishioners to be *ministers* of Christ?" It is not difficult to hand over menial parish duties to laymen, but this is not ministry. It is difficult to equip members to preach, teach, and counsel and then accept gladly their effective ministry to persons whom the ordained minister has not been able to reach. But wherever the clergy and lay officials accept the authority of God's Word and discipline themselves to be obedient to Christ's demands, the Holy Spirit uses their obedience to fashion corporate ministry.

One evidence of a right relationship between the clergy and lay leaders is their mutual confidence in the practice of prayer. Each day the ordained minister prays for his lay leaders and other parishioners by name; and they, discovering what he is about and that prayer is work, pray for one another too. Searching the Scriptures for an authentic image of ministry, dialoguing, and witnessing to one another, first a few and then many leaders

173

committed themselves to the discipline of prayer. Our experience at Trinity convinces us that skillful foremen can build and manage prosperous institutions, but only God's ministers, ordained and lay, can upbuild the people of God. The discipline of private and public prayer, like the disciplined use of Scripture, is essential to upbuilding the people of God. Parish renewal does not happen where pastors and people neglect petitionary and intercessary prayer. There is evidence that many American parishes place more confidence in human plans and attractive programs than in persistent prayer in the name of Christ. It is often true that the American parish has not because it asks not.

Another evidence of a right relationship between the clergy and lay leaders is their mutual willingness to face up to their mistakes in judgment, always to acknowledge them to one another and to the congregation if the admission serves constructive purpose. At the same time parish leaders, equipped to assess and to resist neurotic demands from all corners of the parish, accept the tensions inherent in leadership and in the inevitable conflicts which imaginative leadership breeds. Mistakes are inevitable; but open judgments, clear-cut decisions, and bold deeds by the clerical and lay leaders are an integral part of parish renewal. Only those who live by grace are ever really bold!

A third evidence of a right relationship between the clergy and lay leaders is their mutual interest in and growing commitment to theology as an effective tool for Christ's ministry. The current impasse between theology and activism in the American parish cannot be laid at the door of the laity. The clergy must accept the responsibility. The old cliché in ministerial circles—"But, I'm no theologian"—locates the blame properly. But if the ordained minister views theology as an end in itself, it will

174

insulate him against reality and alienate the laity. Laymen can be interested in theology as a means and trained to use it as a tool, if their shepherd values and employs it so.

Finally, the long, arduous road to parish renewal taught Trinity's clergy and lay leaders the need for patience. We learned to wait for the kingdom as well as work for its coming. There is a residue of Christian judgment and concern in most parishes. It waits to be uncovered; it cannot be forced. Many parishioners will respond to the bold proclamation of the gospel if their freedom is respected while they are accepting God's glorious promises and learning obedience to Christ. Wherever the clergy love persons more than they cherish ideas, doctrines, liturgies, and parish activities; and wherever lay leaders love persons more than they enjoy committee work, bank balances, and chairmanships—congregations discover the secret of being born again.

Staff Responsibilities

Lay and clerical personnel at Trinity share in the full ministry of Christ, but each has his areas of particular responsibility. In the interests of an effective ministry and each man's freedom to be God's minister the responsibilities of the clergy, lay assistant, and minister of music are defined in consultation with them and the vestry. Unless they request it, the senior pastor does not join any of his associates in their areas of primary pastoral responsibility. All pastoral acts, for example, are handled singly by the clergyman who has been invited or delegated to serve. The notion that two or three ordained men need to be present at a funeral service, a marriage ceremony, or a baptism is unwise stewardship of the money which people entrust to the church, a poor evidence of the clergy's mutual confidence in one another, and a sinful concession to ego demands—clerical and lay.

Trinity's staff accepts primary responsibility for particular functions of ministry, but there are no completely specialized ministries—no full-time minister of Christian education, for example. The senior pastor preaches, counsels, teaches, visits, and administers. Another clergyman teaches, visits, preaches, counsels, and administrates; and another evangelizes, teaches, preaches, counsels, and administrates. The lay assistant evangelizes, teaches, visits, counsels, administrates, and preaches. Each man serves singly as staff liaison for several vestry committees. The minister of music teaches in the church school and in the choir camp, evangelizes, and does parish visitation. The clergy, lay assistant, and minister of music meet weekly to coordinate the several functions of ministry and to plan each worship service. Except for the clergy the staff works in cooperation with the lay assistant. The clergy, lay assistant, minister of music, and treasurer submit written monthly reports to the vestry; the committee chairmen report orally; the trustees submit printed semiannual reports. There is order in the parish so that persons are free to proclaim, teach, accept, or reject God's Word.

Auxiliaries

Finally, effective administration in the American parish calls for certain auxiliaries—parish organizations. Unfortunately, too many parishes fondle or tolerate auxiliaries and organizations which, while serving no vital function of Christ's ministry, hinder parish renewal. This mundane reality must be faced. A decade ago, there were a dozen auxiliaries and organized groups in Trinity, each a sovereign state which delimited the ministry of Christ by being a splinter congregation. Today there are three, each responsible to the vestry who review the ministry of each periodically. The United States had a civil war, resolving in blood that sovereignty rests in the federal government. Until the congregation has its "Appomattox Courthouse" on parish organizations—it took seven years at Trinity—it will be hampered severely in its exercise of corporate ministry. Equally, it is ecclesiastical nonsense to assume that every congregation must have the same organizations. Constant vigilance must be exercised to keep parish auxiliaries and organizations from becoming "parish activities" which fragment the church's ministry and insulate church members against the reality of God. Born-again congregations will bury some auxiliaries, only to raise up others which contribute to the exercise of Christ's ministry in the place where they are serving. Diversity can spring from perversity. It also comes spontaneously by the Holy Spirit who employs multiple means to bring persons to Christ.

The administrative procedures in Trinity Church are not precisely like those in First Church, Hackensack, New Jersey, or Christ Church, San Diego, California; they need not be.[1] But any parish seeking to be a vital cell of Christianity honors this principle: traditions, procedures, and methods exist to communicate Christ through persons to persons. Parish renewal requires that all institutional forms be scrutinized regularly and discarded or refashioned and new ones invented with a view to exercising Christ's ministry. The Trinity report demonstrates that the only dynamic resource for Christianizing persons is the

---

[1] There are many practical works on parish administration. See John C. Bramer, *Efficient Church Business Management* (Philadelphia: The Westminster Press, 1960); Paul J. Hoh, *Parish Practice* (Philadelphia: Fortress Press, 1956); Clarence E. Lemmon, *The Art of Church Management* (St. Louis: Bethany Press, 1953).

Word of God and that the human materials are at hand in the parish itself. Institutional forms are needful to the Spirit-filled, corporate ministry. Biblically rooted theology and committed persons employing old and new institutional forms to communicate the Word constitute the church. Without a relevant ministry of the Word, however, there is little to administer in any parish except a social institution fondled by the pious, manipulated by the ecclesiastics, and ignored by the world.

—CHAPTER 8—
IN RETROSPECT

Don't let the world around you squeeze you into its own mold, but let God remold your minds from within. —ROMANS 12:2a (PHILLIPS)

After twelve years of tension and conflict engendered by Trinity's disciplined efforts to accept the demands of Christ and to claim his promises, what images does the parish currently project?

Trinity's New Images

Some view Trinity as a betrayal of the church because its corporate ministry reacts and speaks concretely to political, economic, and social issues. They view this ministry with suspicion —even fear—seeing it as a threat to Lancaster's deep-seated disposition to exalt order above justice. Most members, however, consider this image to be an evidence of Trinity's participation in God's mission. They ask the critics: Is the church a social institution fashioned to secure the interests of a comfortable class of people, or is it a divine instrument of the revolutionary gospel which aims to turn the world right side up? Traditional churchmen in this area can be discomfited by Trinity's flexibility. Members reply, The parish is a means, not an end.

The second image is projected by a *small* corps of Trinity's longtime members who are not comfortable in the new Trinity; they prefer "Old Trinity." Apparently imprisoned by dated emotions which orient them to an idealized yesterday, they recoil from the church as "happening." They want the Trinity of 1920, the Lancaster of 1940, and the laissez-faire politics of 1896. Evidently lacking the emotional resilience to see their cherished views challenged and overmatched by fresh ideas, they have folded their tents and have retired quietly to reminisce, occasionally to brood, but rarely to criticize. They are quiet spectators.

The third image has aroused grave concern among the parish leaders. It is projected by several hundred devoted, hard-working, generous members who, having labored valiantly for more than a decade, feel that Trinity has "arrived." Content with the church's vigorous strides and their intense involvement with God in the renewal of their parish, this substantial bloc is resisting—often unconsciously—the gospel's relentless call, not to excellence, but to perfection. Unchecked, this attitude could breed parish-wide complacency. The parish leaders, having recognized the malady, are probing its psychological and spiritual roots. We suspect that Trinity needs God's judgment and grace more urgently now than it did twelve years ago!

Finally, this current image is dominant: a church presently

"aflame with the Spirit who is the Lord and Giver of life" and valuing "a theology which is . . . passionately missionary." [1] By grace and through obedience Trinity discovered the secret of being born again. By grace and through obedience born-again Trinity is exercising Christ's ministry in and beyond Lancaster *now*. By grace and through obedience Trinity's new life will mature and its witness increase.

Summary Statement

The reader may appreciate a summary statement on this depth study of a 245-year-old parish which discovered the secret of being born again.

I

The American parish, poised geographically for witness and dear to the hearts of many people, can be an effective instrument for exercising Christ's ministry. It is evident that the unconverted church will perish as a finite center in a perishing culture, but the judgment that its demise has taken place is premature. The church could have perished in the sixteenth century; it did not because of inner renewal and outer reform. Parish renewal is possible at mid-twentieth century. The parish's pious platitudes can be tranformed into flaming truth. Its stained glass attitudes can be transformed into fervent love for God's creation. The personnel and machinery to execute God's mission *now* are at hand.

Bypassing the parish is unrealistic; institutional forms are inescapable. The human disposition to over-spiritualize is as unbiblical, and therefore as hurtful, as the disposition to be preoccupied with institutional forms. Committed, knowledge-

[1] James S. Stewart, *A Faith to Proclaim* (New York: Charles Scribner's Sons, 1953), p. 11.

able, sensitive clergy and laity are at work in their parishes, disciplining themselves, reaching into the resources of the Word, orienting to the biblical image of ministry, confident that the Holy Spirit will transform their parish. The fact that the oldest church in the oldest inland city in the United States, located at the center of an urban complex in the heart of the Pennsylvania-Dutch culture, was born again strongly supports the argument that parish renewal is possible today—Chapters 1 and 2.

II

The born-again parish does not disdain institutional forms. It brings them under God's judgment to discern whether they are means or ends, altering and discarding those which do not contribute to the exercise of Christ's ministry. A Spirit-filled ministry, lacking structure and order, must dissipate its force. Christianity has bridged the centuries because it has provided a Spirit-inhabited institution through which the Word becomes flesh in each new generation. Christ's church shapes historical forms through which he can confront persons in time, forms within which it can *be* and through which it can accomplish God's mission. The administration of any parish is sound insofar as it achieves a measure of equilibrium between freedom and discipline. The Holy Spirit's efforts to persuade persons in their freedom to follow Christ are helped or hindered by institutional forms. The born-again parish keeps them under constant scrutiny so that they help rather than hinder—Chapter 7.

III

The impasse between theology and activism in the American parish can be broken. The unconverted parish—a complex of human piety, biblicism, theological naïveté, uncritical devotion to an institution, and parish activities—confronted by the Word in multiple personal encounters, can be transformed by the Holy Spirit into a dynamic community of persons who employ theology as a tool in fashioning the church's effective ministry. A dynamic theology aids in parish renewal; correct or static theology stifles it. But how can any theology be dynamic apart from authentic clerical and lay ministers? And how can the church expect to have authentic ministers without driving to the wellsprings of its life—the person, message, and ministry of Jesus? The historical truth that God was in Jesus of Nazareth is inseparable from the eternal truth that God is in Christ. What Jesus said and did reveals the eternal truth. He is the source for both genuine humanity and authentic ministry.

Parish renewal, therefore, does not happen in those congregations where preaching, teaching, counseling, and administration take not only their techniques but many of their objectives and some of their content from secular sources: pagan rhetoric, clinical and depth psychology, and organization thinking. These secular disciplines and techniques offer insights and methods which, critically applied, aid in the communication of the gospel, strengthen pastoral counseling, improve parish administration, and sharpen Christian theology. But these cultural disciplines are not resources; the church's only resource is God's Word. Gospel preaching, evangelical teaching, and pastoral counseling exist insofar as they testify to and communicate God's saving work in Christ. Apart from the Word they are human activities—Chapters 3, 4, and 5.

IV

A true sense of Christian vocation emerges among the laity when, viewed as subjects rather than objects, they are confronted with the Word in their freedom and equipped from it to witness and serve. The laity can be persuaded to view the priesthood of believers not as a band of spiritual anarchists but as the company of the committed; they can be motivated and equipped from the Word to exercise priestly service to God and man. But this transformation is not likely to happen unless ordained ministers understand lay ministry in the biblical sense, really want it in their parishes, and patiently wait for it as well as work for it. Gospel preaching persuades persons to repent and become disciples. Evangelical teaching equips these disciples to be witnesses and to render priestly service. Christian vocation emerges like "a melody played by ear in the rhythms of twentieth-century life." [2]

But neither laity nor clergy are endowed naturally or equipped easily to witness for Christ and render priestly service. Until both are converted, they are not able to exercise Christ's ministry. And in those parishes where the clerical and lay leaders are concerned primarily to run the church efficiently, the gulf between the church and the world is widened. Those parishes become beehives of irrelevant activities, noisy assemblies with chasmic divisions, or static social clubs. Parish renewal cannot be programmed, packaged, or promoted. The key to it is not in mechanics but in Christian motivation. Conversion, authentic ministry, and parish renewal are inextricably bound together—Chapters 6 and 7.

V

Because the image of ministry entertained and projected by pastors and people affects radically the degree to which the church

[2] *The New Shape of American Religion*, p. 147.

exercises Christ's ministry, it is imperative that both discern and orient to an authentic image. The quest for this image begins not within the context of the profession, but within the context of the faith. Standing humbly before the tribunal of biblical evidence, one discovers that the authentic minister begins as a man—perverse, finite, lost—justified through faith, made new in Christ, but still a man. The Holy Spirit uses this new creature, obedient in his freedom, to communicate the living Word through his freedom. This shepherd-prophet, grateful that he is cared for by Christ, cares for others from Christ's love, confronting them with Christ's demands and promises, and equipping them from the Word to be prophets, teachers, and evangelists.

The authority which prompts this confrontation is not resident in an order, a dogma, or a liturgy; it is in the living Word. Ministry, dogma, and liturgy carry God's authority only when they testify to Christ. No servant of the Word, therefore, directs, manages, or manipulates persons; he knows that the Holy Spirit declines these activities and that the human spirit, although seeming at times to respond to them, cannot escape the implications of human freedom without perverting its essential nature.

Parish renewal is not likely to happen apart from parish pastors who, disciplined in their daily dependence on God to handle the responsibilities of shepherding, are also theologically knowledgeable, emotionally resilient, and intellectually curious. It is unrealistic to assume that the clergy need expect nothing of themselves in leadership which laymen do not expect from themselves. Shepherding is preeminently the ordained minister's task—Chapter 2.

VI

Depth studies of the American parish are a crucial need at this juncture. The parishes are the laboratories where the doctrines of God and man are tested, demonstrated, emasculated, or ignored; where gospel preaching creates conflict and sacrifice, or smooth homilies insulate persons against reality; where evangelical teaching is equipping the saints, or snappy programs are fostering sheer activism; where pastoral counseling is bringing persons to God, or psychological counseling is helping personages to adapt to a depersonalized culture. The parishes are the arenas where persons are discerning life's true meaning in the personhood of Christ and are rendering priestly service in the world for his sake, or where personages, relating casually to their own kind, are escaping rugged encounters with the world. Without these firsthand reports ecclesiastical officials and theologians can get afield of reality.

These vigorous inquiries into the life of particular congregations can be creative in those parishes. They may also prod the church in its efforts to examine and shepherd its ministerial students more realistically and to provide pastoral care for its veterans, to encourage those institutions which are struggling to make theological education relevant, and to contribute something significant to the reformulation of theology.[3] It is true that where imperfect church members wrestle with the Word, God overmatches their imperfections and magnifies their halting acts of obedience to Christ. His Holy Spirit transforms these members into disciples and those disciples into witnesses; the church becomes God's mission to the lost world. That is the testimony of this report.

[3] *The Purpose of the Church and Its Ministry.* See pp. 18, 95-134.

All this may seem insignificant in a nation where people rush wildly one year to build fallout shelters, stand eyeball to eyeball with their adversary the next, and boast the following year that they will be the first to place a man on the moon. But to see how God uses one church to save some people from self-destruction is to see how he can use his church to save the world from annihilation. Salvation is not only eschatological; it is mundane.

BIBLIOGRAPHY

These articles and books have been helpful to the clergy and laity in Trinity Church as they wrestled with God's Word in the agonizing experience of parish renewal. A few laymen can read any of them. Some laymen can read most of them. Most laymen can read several of them.

Contemporary Culture

Allport, Gordon W. *Becoming: Basic Considerations for a Psychology of Personality*. New Haven: Yale University Press, 1955. (This book is excellent background for clergy, teachers, counselors, and parents.)

Barzun, Jacques. *The House of Intellect*. Torchbooks ed.; New York: Harper & Row, 1959. (Every clergyman should read it.)

Bennett, John C. *Christianity and Communism Today*. Reflection Books ed.; New York: Association Press, 1962.

Bennett, John C., editor. *Nuclear Weapons and the Conflict of Conscience*. New York: Charles Scribner's Sons, 1961.

Brill, A. A., editor. *The Basic Writings of Sigmund Freud.* Modern Library ed.; New York: Random House, 1938.

Bruckberger, Raymond L. *The Image of America.* New York: The Viking Press, 1959. (This is a French Dominican priest's attempt to understand "America as a reality"; he offers fresh insights on America and Europe.)

Cailliet, Emile. *The Christian Approach to Culture.* Nashville: Abingdon Press, 1953.

Camus, Albert. *The Fall.* Translated by Justin O'Brien. New York: Alfred A. Knopf, 1957.

————. *The Rebel.* Translated by Anthony Bower. Vintage Books ed.; New York: Random House, 1957.

Curti, Merle. *The Growth of American Thought.* New York: Harper & Row, 1943.

Dawson, Christopher H. *The Historical Reality of Christian Culture.* New York: Harper & Row, 1960. (Especially useful to the clergy.)

Fagley, Richard M. *The Population Explosion and Christian Responsibility.* New York: Oxford University Press, 1960.

Fromm, Erich. *Escape From Freedom.* New York: Holt, Rinehart & Winston, 1941.

Galbraith, John Kenneth. *The Affluent Society.* Boston: Houghton Mifflin Company, 1958.

Gardner, John W. *Excellence: Can We Be Equal and Excellent Too?* New York: Harper & Row, 1961. (Clergy, teachers, and lay leaders.)

————. *Self-Renewal: The Individual and the Innovative.* New York: Harper & Row, 1964. (Clergy and lay leaders.)

Goldman, Eric. *Rendezvous with Destiny.* Vintage Books ed.; New York: Random House, 1956. (This outstanding historical work on America from 1900 through 1950 is now in paperback.)

Hand, Learned. *The Spirit of Liberty.* New York: Alfred A. Knopf, 1952. Vintage Books ed.; New York: Random House, 1960.

Highet, Gilbert. *The Art of Teaching.* Vintage Books ed.; New York: Random House, 1954. (Indispensable to teachers; excellent for parents.)

BIBLIOGRAPHY

Hofstadter, Richard. *Anti-Intellectualism in American Life.* New York: Alfred A. Knopf, 1963. (Every clergyman should read it.)

Hodges, Wayne. *Company and Community: Case Studies in Industry-City Relationships.* New York: Harper & Row, 1958.

Jacob, Philip E. *Changing Values in College.* New York: Harper & Brothers, 1958. (This book presents a sobering challenge to democratic educators.)

Kennan, George F. *Russia and the West Under Lenin and Stalin. The Atlantic Monthly* Press; Boston: Little, Brown and Company, 1961. (Clergy and lay leaders for historical perspective.)

Kohn, Hans. *Nationalism, Its Meaning and History.* Princeton: D. Van Nostrand Co., 1955. (Indispensable for responsible citizenship.)

Maslow, A. H. *Motivation and Personality.* New York: Harper & Row, 1954. (Clergy and lay leaders.)

Morrison, S. E., and Commanger, H. S. *The Growth of the American Republic.* 2 vols.; Rev. ed.; New York: Oxford University Press, 1962. (This is a classic in scholarship and style.)

Niebuhr, H. Richard. *Christ and Culture.* Torchbooks ed.; New York: Harper & Row, 1956. (Chapters 1, 5, and 6 are especially helpful.)

Niebuhr, Reinhold. *Pious and Secular America.* New York: Charles Scribner's Sons, 1958.

_____. *The Nature and Destiny of Man.* 2 vols.; New York: Charles Scribner's Sons, 1941. (Vol. I is a critical evaluation of human nature from the standpoint of the Christian faith and in terms of comparison with alternate interpretations. It belongs in every clergyman's library and in some laymen's libraries.)

Northrop, F. S. C. *The Meeting of East and West.* Macmillan Paperbacks ed.; New York: The Macmillan Company, 1960.

Packard, Vance. *The Hidden Persuaders.* New York: David McKay Co., 1957.

Randall, John Herman, Jr. *The Making of the Modern Mind.* Rev. ed.; New York: Houghton Mifflin Company, 1940.

Riesman, David. *The Lonely Crowd.* New Haven: Yale University Press, 1950.

191

Sartre, Jean-Paul. *The Devil and the Good Lord*. Vintage Books ed.; New York: Random House, 1962.

Tawney, R. H. *Religion and the Rise of Capitalism*. London: Penguin Books, Inc., 1947.

Tocqueville, Alexis de. *Democracy in America*. Translated by Phillips Bradley. 2 vols.; New York: Alfred A. Knopf, 1944.

Ward, Barbara. *Five Ideas That Change the World*. New York: W. W. Norton & Company, 1959. (This is a concise presentation on nationalism, industrialism, colonialism, communism, and internationalism.)

Whyte, William. *The Organization Man*. New York: Simon and Schuster, 1956. (This is an up-to-date study until automation replaces the organization man or until the church persuades him to a higher allegiance.)

The clergy and laity, constrained to creative dialogue with one another and the world, will reach for many publications—*The Atlantic Monthly, Saturday Review, The Christian Century, Christianity and Crisis, Christianity Today, The Nation, The New Republic, Religion in Life, Commonweal, The Catholic World, Dialogue,* the Sunday edition of *The New York Times,* and others. They will sample twentieth-century fiction and drama by James Baldwin, Saul Bellow, James Cozzens, T. S. Eliot, William Faulkner, Herbert Gold, Graham Greene, Ernest Hemingway, J. P. Marquand, Mary McCarthy, Arthur Miller, George Orwell, John O'Hara, J. D. Salinger, John Updike, Tennessee Williams, Sloane Wilson, Herman Wouk, Robert Penn Warren, and others. The Bible, now in multiple translations and styles, is the one indispensable book as this report on parish renewal makes plain.

The Parish

PAMPHLETS AND ARTICLES

Blizzard, Samuel W. "A Young Minister's Dilemma," *The Christian Century,* April 25, 1956. (Laity.)

Erikson, Erik H. "The Problem of Ego Identity," *Journal of the American Psychoanalytical Association,* January, 1956. (Counselors and teachers.)

"Help Wanted: Ministers, Priests, and Rabbis," *Look,* November 20, 1962. (Laity.)

Lynes, Russel. "Time on Our Hands," *Harper's*, July, 1958. (Laity.)

MacKinnon, Donald W. "The Nature and Nurture of Creative Talent," *American Psychologist*, July, 1962. (Clergy and lay leaders.)

Pearson, Roy. "Don't Blame the Laymen!" *The Pulpit* (November, 1961). (Clergy.)

Sittler, Joseph A. "Called to Unity," *The Ecumenical Review*, January, 1962. (Clergy and official boards.)

Symposium on the Lay Renaissance. *Religion in Life*, Winter, 1961-62. (Clergy and laity.)

BOOKS

Albright, William F. *From the Stone Age to Christianity*. Anchor Books ed.; 2nd ed.; Garden City: Doubleday & Company, 1957.

Aulén, Gustaf. *The Faith of the Christian Church*. Rev. ed.; Philadelphia: Fortress Press, 1961. (Clergy.)

Baillie, John. *Diary of Private Prayer*. New York: Charles Scribner's Sons, 1949. (Clergy and laity.)

Bainton, Roland H. *Here I Stand*. Nashville: Abingdon Press, 1950.

Baxter, Richard. *The Reformed Pastor*. Richmond: John Knox Press, 1963. (This is a seventeenth-century classic which is sharply relevant today.)

Berger, Peter. *The Noise of Solemn Assemblies*. Garden City: Doubleday & Company, 1961. (This is a sobering critique by a sociologist.)

Boisen, Anton T. *The Exploration of the Inner World*. Torchbooks ed.; New York: Harper & Row, 1962. (Pastoral counselors.)

Bonhoeffer, Dietrich. *The Cost of Discipleship*. Translated by R. H. Fuller. 2nd rev. ed.; New York: The Macmillan Company, 1960. (Clergy and laity.)

Bretall, Robert, editor. *A Kierkegaard Anthology*. Princeton: Princeton University Press, 1946.

Bridston, Keith R., and Culver, Dwight W., editors. *The Making of Ministers*. Minneapolis: Augsburg Publishing House, 1964.

Brown, Robert McAfee. *The Significance of the Church*. Philadelphia: The Westminster Press, 1956.

Brunner, Emil H. *The Misunderstanding of the Church.* Philadelphia: The Westminster Press, 1953.

Calvin, John. *Institutes of the Christian Religion.* Edited by John T. McNeill. 2 vols.; Philadelphia: The Westminster Press, 1960.

Clark, Elmer T. *The Small Sects in America.* Rev. ed.; Apex ed.; Nashville: Abingdon Press, 1949.

Cullmann, Oscar. *The State in the New Testament.* New York: Charles Scribner's Sons, 1956.

Davies, D. R. *Secular Illusion or Christian Realism?* 2nd ed. rev.; New York: The Macmillan Company, 1953. (A concise, hard-hitting little book for clergy, lay leaders, and evangelists.)

Dix, Gregory. *The Shape of the Liturgy.* Naperville, Ill.: Alec R. Allenson, 1960. (Clergy.)

Doniger, Simon, editor. *The Nature of Man in Theological and Psychological Perspective.* New York: Harper & Row, 1962. (Counselors and teachers.)

Ebeling, Gerhard. *Word and Faith.* Philadelphia: Fortress Press, 1963. (Ebeling is a notably creative theologian; this is an indispensable book for the clergy.)

_____. *The Nature of Faith.* Philadelphia: Fortress Press, 1961.

Fairchild, Roy W., and Wynn, John C. *Families in the Church: A Protestant Survey.* New York: Association Press, 1961.

Farmer, Herbert H. *The Servant of the Word.* Philadelphia: Fortress Press, 1964. (Basic for lay preachers and teachers.)

Frakes, Margaret. *Bridges to Understanding.* Philadelphia: Fortress Press, 1960.

Gilmore, G. Don. *In the Midst.* Grand Rapids: Wm. B. Eerdmans Publishing Co., 1962. (Discusses renewal through small groups.)

Godsey, John D. *The Theology of Dietrich Bonhoeffer.* Philadelphia: The Westminster Press, 1960.

Goodall, Norman. *The Ecumenical Movement.* London: Oxford University Press, 1964.

Haselden, Kyle. *The Racial Problem in Christian Perspective.* Torchbooks ed.; New York: Harper & Row, 1959. (Laity.)

Heim, Karl. *Christian Faith and Natural Science*. New York: Harper & Brothers, 1953.

Heinecken, Martin J. *The Moment Before God*. Philadelphia: Fortress Press, 1956. (Treats Kierkegaard as a Christian—useful to counselors.)

Herberg, Will. *Protestant—Catholic—Jew*. Anchor Book ed.; Garden City: Doubleday & Company, 1955.

Hiltner, Seward. *Preface to Pastoral Theology*. Nashville: Abingdon Press, 1958.

Hochhuth, Rolf. *The Deputy*. Translated by Richard and Clara Winston. New York: Grove Press, 1964. (Clergy and laymen should wrestle with the complete text of the drama.)

Hofmann, Hans, editor. *Making the Ministry Relevant*. New York: Charles Scribner's Sons, 1960.

Hulme, William E. *Counseling and Theology*. Philadelphia: Fortress Press, 1956.

Hunter, A. M. *Introducing the New Testament*. Rev. ed.; Philadelphia: The Westminster Press, 1958. (Lay teachers.)

The Interpreter's Bible. 12 vols.; Nashville: Abingdon Press, 1952-57. (Belongs in *every* parish library.)

Jackson, Edgar N. *Understanding Grief*. Nashville: Abingdon Press, 1957.

Johnson, Paul E. *Psychology of Pastoral Care*. Nashville: Abingdon Press, 1953.

Kraemer, Hendrik. *A Theology of the Laity*. Philadelphia: The Westminster Press, 1958. (Clergy and lay leaders especially.)

Latourette, Kenneth Scott. *The Christian World Mission in Our Day*. New York: Harper & Brothers, 1954.

Lazareth, William H. *Man: In Whose Image*. Philadelphia: Fortress Press, 1961. (Laity.)

Lee, Robert, editor. *Cities and Churches: Readings on the Urban Church*. Philadelphia: The Westminster Press, 1962.

Lee, Robert, and Marty, Martin E., editors. *Religion and Social Conflict*. New York: Oxford University Press, 1964. (Clergy and official boards.)

Lehmann, Paul. *Ethics in a Christian Context*. New York: Harper & Row, 1963. (Clergy.)

Leibrecht, Walter. *Being a Christian in Today's World*. Philadelphia: Fortress Press, 1962. (Excellent for the laity.)

Lewis, C. S. *The Screwtape Letters & Screwtape Proposes a Toast*. Macmillan Paperbacks ed.; New York: The Macmillan Company, 1962. (Laity.)

Luther, Martin. *Early Theological Works*. Edited by James Atkinson. Philadelphia: The Westminster Press, 1962.

Marty, Martin E. *The New Shape of American Religion*. New York: Harper & Row, 1959.

Miller, William L. *The Protestant and Politics*. Philadelphia: The Westminster Press, 1958. (A basic book for laymen.)

Minear, Paul S. *Images of the Church in the New Testament*. Philadelphia: The Westminster Press, 1960. (Clergy and lay teachers.)

Neill, Stephen C., and Weber, Hans-Ruedi, editors. *The Layman in Christian History*. Philadelphia: The Westminster Press, 1963. (This is the first comprehensive work in the field and is excellent for clergy and lay leaders.)

Niebuhr, H. Richard. *The Purpose of the Church and Its Ministry*. New York: Harper & Row, 1956. (Belongs in every parish library.)

Niebuhr, Reinhold. *Faith and History*. New York: Charles Scribner's Sons, 1949.

Niebuhr, Reinhold, consulting editor. *Christian Faith Series*. Garden City: Doubleday & Company, 1955—.

Raines, Robert A. *New Life in the Church*. New York: Harper & Row, 1961. (States the need for conversion in the parish.)

Read, David H. C. *The Christian Faith*. New York: Charles Scribner's Sons, 1956. (A solid, brief statement.)

Richardson, Alan. *The Gospel and Modern Thought*. New York: Oxford University Press, 1950. (Lay teachers and evangelists.)

Roberts, David E. *Existentialism and Religious Belief*. Galaxy ed.; New York: Oxford University Press, 1957. (Clergy and college-educated laity.)

Routley, Erik. *The Gift of Conversion*. Philadelphia: Fortress Press, 1958.

————. *Hymns and Faith*. Greenwich: The Seabury Press, 1956.

Rutenborn, Guenter. *The Sign of Jonah*. New York: Thomas Nelson & Sons, 1960.

Sangster, W. E. *Power in Preaching*. Nashville: Abingdon Press, 1958.

Scherer, Paul. *For We Have This Treasure*. New York: Harper & Brothers, 1944. (This is a giant in the distinguished series of Beecher Lectures at Yale.)

Smart, James D. *The Teaching Ministry of the Church*. Philadelphia: The Westminster Press, 1954. (Biblical and theological—very useful.)

Stewart, James S. *A Faith to Proclaim*. New York: Charles Scribner's Sons, 1953. (Another giant in the Beecher Lecture series on the "essential message of our evangelism rather than on its manner or method.")

Stone, Hannah M. and Abraham. *A Marriage Manual*. Rev. ed.; New York: Simon and Schuster, 1962. (Basic for premarriage counseling; many couples should obtain a copy.)

Tappert, Theodore G., editor. *The Book of Concord*. Philadelphia: Fortress Press, 1959.

Thielicke, Helmut. *The Ethics of Sex*. New York: Harper & Row, 1964. (This is the best work in the field; it should be shared widely in the parish.)

Thurneysen, Eduard. *A Theology of Pastoral Care*. Richmond: John Knox Press, 1962. (This presents a substantial, continental slant by Barth's lifelong colleague.)

Tillich, Paul. *The Courage to Be*. New Haven: Yale University Press, 1952.

————. *The New Being*. New York: Charles Scribner's Sons, 1955.

————. *Systematic Theology*. 3 vols.; Chicago: University of Chicago Press, 1951-63.

Tournier, Paul. *The Meaning of Persons*. New York: Harper & Row, 1957. (Ideally every parishioner and clergyman should study Parts I and III— "The Personage" and "The Person.")

Trueblood, D. Elton. *The Company of the Committed*. New York: Harper & Row, 1961. (Excellent for the laity.)

Watson, Philip S. *Let God Be God! An Interpretation of the Theology of Martin Luther*. Philadelphia: Fortress Press, 1947. (Clergy and laity.)

Weatherhead, Leslie D. *Psychology, Religion, and Healing*. Apex ed.; Nashville: Abingdon Press, 1951. (A rich resource book for pastoral counselors.)

_____. *Over His Own Signature*. Nashville: Abingdon Press, 1955. (Any layman will profit from it.)

Weber, Hans-Ruedi, editor. *Signs of Renewal*. Geneva: World Council of Churches, 1957.

Williams, Daniel D. *The Minister and the Care of Souls*. New York: Harper & Row, 1961. (Clergy.)

Wingren, Gustaf. *Theology in Conflict*. Translated by Eric H. Wahlstrom. Philadelphia: Fortress Press, 1958. (Clergy and lay teachers.)

_____. *Luther on Vocation*. Translated by Carl C. Rasmussen. Philadelphia: Fortress Press, 1957.

Wright, G. Ernest, and Fuller, Reginald H. *The Book of the Acts of God*. Garden City: Doubleday & Company, 1957. (Lay teachers.)

INDEX

Beecher, Henry Ward, 52
benevolence: money for, 121, 138-39, 166; "second mile," 172
Bennett, John C., 97, 99
Berger, Peter, 67, 68
Bible: as channel of God's grace, 59; image of ministry in, 41-47, 49, 162; read in the light of Christ, 91; sermons oriented to, 56-59; as witness to God's activity, 23
Bible School, 58, 71. See also church school
Bible study, 89-92, 109
board, official: election of, 169-70; transformation of, 169-75
Bonhoeffer, Dietrich, 92, 99, 103
Book of the Acts of God, The (Wright and Fuller), 97
Book of Concord, The (Tappert, ed.), 97
book reviews, 92-94
"Books and Coffee," 93-94
Bossard, James H. S., 150 n.
Bowie, Walter Russell, 115 n.
Boy Scouts, 141
Bramer, John C., 177 n.
Brilioth, Yngve, 128 n.
Bruce, A. B., 73
Bruckberger, R. L., 51 n., 92, 97, 98, 99
Brunner, Emil, 51 n.
Burtness, James H., 144 n.
Butterfield, Herbert, 51 n.
Buttrick, George A., 51 n., 73

Calvin, John, 97, 128
Camus, Albert, 97, 98, 99, 104
canteen, teen-age, 87-88, 141
Carlyle, 103

catechetical instruction, 84-86, 153
Catholic—Protestant—Jew (Herberg), 52 n.
Chalmers, Thomas, 52
children: in church life, 127; church school for, 71-77. See also youth
choirs, 166, 167
Christ and Culture (Niebuhr), 52 n., 104 n.
Christian Faith Series, 97
Christian fellowship. See koinonia
Christian Shepherd, The (Hiltner), 147 n.
Christian vocation, 21, 153, 183-84
Christian World Mission in Our Day, The (Latourette), 104 n.
Christianity and Civilisation (Brunner), 51 n.
Christianity and Communism Today (Bennett), 97
Christianity and History (Butterfield), 51 n.
church; attendance at, 108, 117; children's 127; concept of, as "happening," 19, 23; history of, 126; work of, as escape from God, 45, 177
church school: 57, 58; adult, 77-84; for children, 71-77; teenage participation in, 86-87
Churchill, Winston, 98
Clark, Elmer T., 97
classes, social, in America, 140
clergy: challenges to preaching of, 60; close scrutiny of, 158; emotional health of, 159; place of, 45-46; relationship of laity and, 109, 173-75; responsibilities of,

203